NAME: SPIDER-MAN™

SECRET IDENTITY:
Peter Parker

ABILITY POINTS:

Fighting:	6
Agility:	10
Strength:	8
Endurance:	8
Reason:	4
Intuition:	10
Psyche:	8
Agility with Webbing:	16

KARMA POINTS: 12

—— —— —— —— ——

—— —— —— —— ——

HEALTH POINTS: 32

—— —— —— —— ——

—— —— —— —— ——

—— —— —— —— ——

—— —— —— —— ——

THE AMAZING SPIDER-MAN
in
AS THE WORLD BURNS

BUT HE DOESN'T EXIST!

"You've come a long way, Spider-Man, to meet your death!" the Hobgoblin laughs.

He's not the real article, you tell yourself. He's just plucked from my memories. But he can kill me just as dead.

You fire your webbing at him as fast as you can. Your web shot is right on the mark, covering Hobby's weapons bag, as well as his midsection.

"You think to stop me with this puny weapon?!" he howls.

"Nah, I've got lots more puny weapons – like my spider-strength and –"

Suddenly, you hear a train approaching, and feel the earth beneath your feet begin to rumble. Realizing the possibilities, you check to make sure your feet are solidly anchored to the floor. Nothing can make you unstick against your will. Bracing yourself, you swing the pseudo-Hobgoblin into the path of the oncoming train.

Have you got the strength to eliminate
this deadly apparition of the Hobgoblin?

Make a Strength FEAT roll, adding Karma if you wish. If the result is 12 or less, go to **140**. If it is 13 or more, go to **121**.

Whatever the outcome, only your decisions, and the luck of the dice roll, can help you find the person responsible for your fate, **As the World Burns.**

Adventure Gamebook # 6

AS THE WORLD BURNS

Peter David

Illustrated by John Statema
and Mark Nelson

PUFFIN BOOKS
in association with TSR, Inc.

PUFFIN BOOKS

Published by the Penguin Group
27 Wrights Lane, London W8 5TZ, England
Viking Penguin Inc., 40 West 23rd Street, New York, New York 10010, USA
Penguin Books Australia Ltd, Ringwood, Victoria, Australia
Penguin Books Canada Ltd, 2801 John Street, Markham, Ontario, Canada L3R 1B4
Penguin Books (NZ) Ltd, 182–190 Wairau Road, Auckland 10, New Zealand

Penguin Books Ltd, Registered Offices: Harmondsworth, Middlesex, England

Created and first published in the USA by TSR, Inc.,
Lake Geneva, Wisconsin 1987
Published in Puffin Books 1989
1 3 5 7 9 10 8 6 4 2

Copyright © Marvel Entertainment Group, Inc., 1987
The Amazing Spider-man™ in *As the World Burns* by
Peter David copyright © Marvel Entertainment Group, Inc., 1987
All rights reserved

The names of characters used herein are fictitious and do not refer to any persons living
or dead. Any descriptions, including similarities to persons living or dead, are merely
coincidental. All Marvel characters, character names, and the distinctive likenesses
thereof, are trademarks of the Marvel Entertainment Group, Inc.

Printed and bound in Great Britain by
Cox & Wyman Ltd, Reading

Except in the United States of America,
this book is sold subject to the condition
that it shall not, by way of trade or otherwise,
be lent, re-sold, hired out, or otherwise circulated
without the publisher's prior consent in any form of
binding or cover other than that in which it is
published and without a similar condition
including this condition being imposed
on the subsequent purchaser

FACE FRONT, TRUE BELIEVERS!

You are about to assume the role of the Amazing Spider-Man and encounter some of the most nefarious villains of the Marvel Universe in an exciting, totally new kind of role-playing game-book.

Based on the popular MARVEL SUPER HEROES Role-Playing Game from TSR, Inc., MARVEL SUPER HEROES Adventure Gamebooks require only a single standard, six-sided die; a pen or pencil; a moderate supply of luck; and, most of all, your own personal skill in making decisions as you play the game. If dice are unavailable, a simple alternative, requiring only pencil and paper, may be used instead. See page 12.

MARVEL SUPER HEROES Adventure Gamebooks have been designed to read easily, without complicated rules to slow down the story. Once you finish reading the rules that follow, you should seldom find it necessary to refer back to them. Your choices are clearly stated at each choice point, with occasional reminders of additional options you have available.

Your adventure reads like a book, plays like a game, and offers a thrill a minute—with YOU as your favorite Marvel Super Hero!

YOUR CHARACTER

In this book, you are the Amazing Spider-Man—
in real life, free-lance photographer Peter Parker.
While you were still in high school, you attended a
demonstration of the safe uses of radioactivity. At
this demonstration, you were accidentally bitten
by a spider that had been exposed to an extremely
high level of radiation. The spider's venom inter-
mingled with your blood, endowing you with the
proportional strength and agility of a spider. In
addition, you acquired a special "spider-sense"
that warns you of danger, along with the incredible ability to cling to walls and ceilings.

Seeking to find a way to support yourself with
your new special abilities, you used your knowledge of chemistry to develop a chemical webbing
that, though easily applied, quickly hardens to a
strong, flexible adhesive binding. So armed, you
set out to make a name in show business, hiding
your natural shyness behind a mask.

Your show business career was short-lived,
however. After one early performance, you failed
to capture a burglar, who later killed your beloved
Uncle Ben. At that point, you learned the hardest
lesson of your life—that with great power comes
great responsibility.

Since that fateful day, you have fought evil and crime wherever and whenever you have found it. Your domain is high above the city, where you swing from building to building on your special weblines. You have battled many formidable foes. Sandman, Electro, Doctor Octopus, Vulture, and the Kingpin of Crime all count you as their enemy. You are feared by many, as a result of inflammatory editorials about you written by newspaper publisher J. Jonah Jameson. However, others have come to know you as a trusted crimefighter and a force for good in the world as you seek to protect the lives of the innocent. . . .

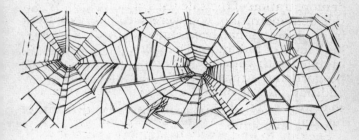

PLAYING THE GAME

The Marvel Super Heroes portrayed in this series of books have certain powerful abilities far beyond those of the average human being. As Spider-Man, your special abilities, which will allow you to attempt things a normal person wouldn't even consider, are listed on the removable Stats Card located at the front of this book. The Stats Card lists everything you need to keep track of in order to play the game in this book. At the same time, it doubles as a handy bookmark.

SCORING

Playing the game requires that you keep track of three things—**Ability points, Karma points**, and **Health points**—on the Super Hero Stats Card located at the front of the book. An explanation of each of these follows.

HEALTH POINTS

Health Points represent your general health or life strength. If you are injured or become ill, you lose some of these points. If you lose all your Health points, you will fall unconscious and possibly even die. At any rate, if your Health points drop to zero or less, your adventure is over. If you are hurt or sick, you may regain some or all of your Health points by healing or by spending Karma, which is explained in the following section. Always remember, however, that it is not possible to regain more health points than you had at the start of the game.

Spider-Man begins this adventure with a total of 32 Health points.

KARMA POINTS

Karma points represent the effects your actions will have on your future. You earn Karma by doing heroic deeds, by making the right decisions, and in general by being a good person. Conversely, if you do things you shouldn't, you may lose Karma. There is no limit to the number of Karma points you can earn, but you will do better to spend your Karma than to hoard it.

You may spend Karma on any die roll you make to increase your chance of success. Here's how it works:

8

You must make your decision to spend Karma *before* you roll the die.

Once you commit yourself to spend Karma on a die roll, you *must* spend at least 2 Karma points. You may add as many more Karma points as you need to make your die roll successful, providing you have enough Karma points to spend. If you decide to spend Karma on your die roll but fail the roll because you didn't have enough Karma points to spend or because you chose not to spend that much Karma, you still lose the original 2 Karma points.

Karma may also be spent to regain lost Health points whenever you reach a choice point in the story. For every Karma point you decide to spend in this manner, increase your total Health score by 1 point. Be sure to subtract the same number from your Karma total. The reverse is not true, however. Health points may *not* be converted to Karma points.

Spider-Man begins this adventure with a total of 12 Karma points.

ABILITY POINTS

Ability points determine how easy or difficult it is for you to perform certain actions, called **FEATS**. Whenever you are asked to attempt a particular type of FEAT, consult the ability called for on your Super Hero Stats Card, roll one die, and add the result of the die roll to your Ability score. The text will indicate what you should do next, according to what your total was.

The abilities used in this gamebook are described below.

FIGHTING determines how good you are in armed and unarmed combat. Your natural skill, combined with your many years as a crimefighter, gives you a much better than average skill with your fists.

AGILITY is a measure of your coordination. The radioactive spider that bit you gave you the proportional agility of a spider, allowing you to dodge and leap great distances, as well as hurl objects with great accuracy.

STRENGTH determines how much damage you inflict when you hit something. It also tells how much weight you are able to lift. You have the proportional strength of a spider, allowing you to lift great weights. You often pull your punches, however, in order to avoid seriously injuring human opponents.

ENDURANCE measures how long you can exert yourself physically without resting. It also determines how well you can stand up to punishment, how long you can hold your breath, and how well you are able to resist the effects of knockout gas. Your Endurance is far beyond that of an ordinary human being—a definite advantage when you go

10

up against powerful villains such as Doctor Doom.

REASON reflects how well you can solve problems with your mind. You have a college education, and you did some graduate work in chemistry before becoming a free-lance photographer, so you're no dummy.

INTUITION gauges how well you observe with your senses and are able to act on that knowledge. Your special spider-sense, gained from your encounter with the radioactive spider, helps make you aware of potential danger, even danger that you cannot directly see.

PSYCHE is based on your willpower and inner strength. A high Psyche score helps you to resist magic and mind control techniques. Your Psyche is far above average for human beings.

AGILITY WITH WEBBING is a special ability that is yours alone. You have developed an incredibly strong temporary adhesive that you can shoot from special web-shooters you wear on your wrists. Through long practice with these web-shooters, you are more comfortable using them than any other weapon. You carry extra cartridges of web-fluid in your belt, along with a mini-camera and a supply of spider-tracers, which are special devices that send out signals tuned to attract your spider-sense.

PLAYING WITHOUT DICE

Should you ever wish to play the adventure when dice are unavailable, there is a simple substitute that requires only pencil and paper. Simply write the numbers 1 through 6 on separate slips of paper and mix them up in a container. When a FEAT roll is called for, draw one of the slips, note the number, and place it back in the container. Mix the numbers up before you draw again. Each draw represents one roll of a die.

You, as Spider-Man, are now ready to face danger and travel around the globe, AS THE WORLD BURNS. Turn to page 13 to begin your adventure. Good luck, and good choices!

You're swinging high over Manhattan, firing **1** weblines with practiced ease from your webshooters. The city is sparkling around you, not a hint of grime or dirt anywhere, as if someone had come through the night before with a mop and pail the size of Rhode Island.

Far below you, the people are waving and pointing. So often in the past, they've hurled jeers and taunts at you, but today there seems to be a note of enthusiasm. Even cheer. Intrigued, you swing down toward them and they're waiting, waving banners, flags with your web-masked face on them and shouting over and over, "Spidey, Spidey, he's our man! If he can't beat 'em, no one can!"

Grinning under your mask, you drop down to accept their accolades. Women are holding up their infants, swaddled in blankets of red and blue with black web lines on them. Men want to shake your hand, and kids want to form fan clubs for you.

Then, pushing through, comes your most frequent nemesis, J. Jonah Jameson, publisher of the *Daily Bugle*. J.J. is chomping down furiously on his cigar, and yet mysteriously it stays in place, as Jonah shouts, "One side, everybody! Let me through! I'm J. Jonah Jameson, and I want to say something to our friend here."

You're slightly taken aback as you say, "Friend? Jonah, ever since I first showed up, you've been on me like a barnacle. What's with the turnaround."

"Ah, Spidey—can I call you Spidey?"

"No," you reply.

"Great. Spidey," he steamrolls, "it's about time I came clean. I've always done that to sell newspa-

14

pers. *Spider-Man: Menace* always reads so much better than *Spider-Man: Swell Guy*, right? But I can't do it to you anymore. I'm here to tell everyone," and Jonah makes a grand gesture, encompassing the crowd, "that I owe my life a hundred times over to this man. And it's time we started treating him like the hero he is, rather than the creep we've always accused him of being."

You're pleased and flabbergasted as Jonah waves his cigar, the smell of the cheap Cuban import pervading the air. "Ring out the bells for Spider-Man!" he shouts.

All around you are the sounds of bells, ringing true and clear, and it's as if they're saying, "Spider-Man—hero!" over and over again. You wave your arms to the crowd, take a step forward—and roll out of bed.

The uncompromising hardness of the floor jolts you awake. You sit up, blinking, on the bare floor, and look around for the crowds. The dreary number readouts from your clock-radio inform you that it's 9:30 in the morning. You've slept later than you have in weeks, and yet you feel as if it weren't enough.

"A dream," you moan. "It figures. I'm the only guy in the world whose waking hours are the ones with nightmares in them."

And then a soft female voice says, "Come on now, Tiger. We haven't been married all that long. Is the bloom off the rose already?"

You peer up over the edge of the bed and Mary Jane Watson-Parker is lying there under the sheets, chin propped up with one hand. She's looking at you with some degree of amusement.

"Is it that bad?" she clucks sympathetically, sighing and stretching herself out. "Is waking up

15

with me really like waking up with the Bride of Frankenstein—and remember, if it is, think about what that makes you."

You grin. You can't help yourself.

"Lucky for you," you say, "I'm feeling kind of monstrous today." You start to climb back into bed.

At that moment, it suddenly dawns on you that the bells you heard in your dream weren't just in your dream. They were part of some overall commotion that's still going on. Because now you're hearing sirens—police sirens, you realize, and as you go to the window and peer out, sure enough, several police cars streak by.

Something's definitely going on, you think to yourself. But then you glance back at your nice warm bed. Whatever's going on, the police can probably take care of it, right?

If you decide to climb back into bed, proceed to **153**. If, however, you can't resist the siren call of danger, leap to **102**.

2   You blink into the brightness of the sun and realize that you're now in Rome—not a tremendously tricky deduction, because even you can recognize the structure looming in front of you— the Roman Coliseum.

Centuries ago, people fought for their lives here. Now it looks barren, except for the tour group that is just leaving. The tourists glance at you, and you think, *Obviously, they believe I'm some idiot in a costume.* Then it occurs to you that they're probably right.

Well, you think. *I must have been dropped near*

16

the Coliseum for a reason—and it's not to star in a remake of Ben Hur.

You wait until the tour bus pulls away, then bound over to the Coliseum. You quickly find a way in—but a place would have to be locked up pretty tight to keep you out.

Go to **201**.

"I may not get another chance," you say, as **3** you bound toward the emperor. The crowd roars as it sees where you're heading, and the emperor blanches, shouting for the guards.

You reach the wall effortlessly, and leap toward him, but there are already a dozen centurions surrounding the emperor. They brandish swords, shields and spears.

It will take you several seconds to fight your way through them—and more centurions, weapons out, are pouring in from all sides.

This is not going to work, you think. At that moment, you hear the thudding of the Rhino behind you.

You turn, and once again he's charging toward Mary Jane.

Go to **130**.

The day I can't smash through a door is the **4** *day I pack it in,* you think to yourself, as the chains snap under the impact of your spider-strength. The door flies open and fresh air—or at least what passes for it in New York—welcomes you.

You're at the rear of the building, and the fire door leads onto a metal stairway. Without hesita-

17

tion, you leap off—a three-story drop is nothing to you, and you land so gently that the woman in your arms is unaware of any impact.

She's trembling from her brush with death, and you're not in any great shape either. But she can't tell, since that's the joy of wearing a full mask. You run around to the front of the building.

Go to **50**.

5 You shake your head to clear it. "Let's try that again, Hobby," you say. You aim your webbing . . . and discover that all you manage to obtain is a pathetic "thwizzing" sound. Your web shooters are slightly bent—no webbing is able to pass through the nozzles. It'll only take you a few minutes to repair the damage—but minutes you just don't have.

Go to **76**.

6 Hurling yourself against the door, you realize you've badly misjudged just how much strength the fire has taken out of you. You knock the door half off its hinges but that's all you're able to manage before you slide to the ground, the world swirling about you.

The next thing you know is that you're being lifted up by assorted hands and carried out of the building. Fresh air starts to bring you around as you're being wildly jostled, and now you know what's happened. The firefighters chopped their way in and managed to keep you from becoming spectacular spider-hash.

Boy, oh boy, you think to yourself, *did I bungle this one.* You're absolutely right. You lose 2 Karma

18

points for getting into this fix in the first place.

The firefighters carry you around to the front of the building. Out of the corner of your eye, you see the shaken woman in the arms of another rescuer.

Then an annoyed-looking man stands over you. Go to **50**.

7

You pull yourself together and start toward the Hulk, regaining strength with every step.

"Didn't have enough, did you?" says the Hulk.

"Funny," you say, with more bravado than brains, "I was about to say the same thing about you."

The Hulk tenses, ready to leap at you.

"Whoa, deja vu," you think to yourself.

Go to **45**.

8

Doc seems a little spacey—then again, he's obviously got a lot on his mind. This whole thing is affecting him, maybe more than he wants to let on. Well, the last thing he needs is you adding to his headaches by voicing your concerns.

"Here you go, Doc," you say cheerfully, tossing him the amulet.

The moment he catches it, you know that you've just made a hideous mistake. A wild cackle fills the house.

Go to **118**.

9

The most important thing is for you to get some time to sort all of this out. And the way to do it is for Spider-Man to disappear for a while.

You swing off toward home and, minutes later, arrive at the skylight.

You lift it open, and steam rises up from inside. At first, you get nervous—*what the devil's happening in there?* But from down in the bathroom, Mary Jane calls out, "Would you mind closing that, please? It's chilly."

Hoo boy, MJ is in the shower, and the steam is rising up and out of the skylight. Quickly, you drop into the bathroom, shutting the skylight behind you. You pull off your mask as you sag down onto the couch, wondering what the devil you should do now.

And at that moment, floating outside your window you see a slim form. You stumble back in shock. Your spider-sense isn't giving any warning at all, but something could again be interfering somehow.

You back up and run into the bathroom. "Gotta go, hon'," you say quickly, as you leap toward the skylight.

"What? But you just—"

You don't even slow down as you leap out onto the roof.

Go to **109**.

"I'm not going to spend my whole life run- **10** ning from you refugees from *Ghostbusters*," you say angrily as you leap straight for the ghost.

It grabs at you, sending a chill through your soul, as your body passes to the other side through it.

You fire a webline, swinging back onto the wall only several stories lower as the ghost drops down toward you. It looks somewhat surprised, but not half as surprised as when it is suddenly enveloped by a ball of mystic energy. It looks around for the source, but doesn't find it soon enough. Within seconds, the gleaming translucent form becomes black and crispened. Moments later, it vanishes into nothingness.

"Nice try, Spider-Man," you hear a lilting voice say.

Go to **99**.

11 The first thing you notice is the change in temperature—instead of the freezing winds of the Himalayas surging around you, you feel the warmer, still air of Doc's Greenwich Village home!

"Fools!" a gutteral voice curses behind you.

You spin around, your spider-sense buzzing.

It's Mordo. At this point, he's not even bothering to try to hide his actual appearance. He's much huskier than Doc is, and far more sinister. He has a short, cropped beard and a high forehead. He's dressed in green, with a high, forked collar and a flowing green cape.

"Didn't you realize?" he says. "I was telling the truth—in a fashion. I was being kept prisoner here, by a spell cast by Strange before I imprisoned him with the power of the quarter-amulet I captured. But the quarter wasn't powerful enough to get rid of Strange's confounded binding spell. Even in his frozen state, he still fights me. Even with the quarter of the Caputo amulet in my grasp, I don't have the power to destroy him or break out of his spells!" Then Mordo leers evilly. "But all that is about to change. You see, Strange is still fighting to maintain his binding spell on me—but others could come and go as they pleased—or as I pleased. So I got your unwitting help, Spider-Man, to obtain the other three parts of the amulet. And with the full amulet in my possession, I'll be able to do anything. Anything!"

"Where's Doc!" you shout.

"Right behind you," Mordo replies.

You spin around to see Doc floating there. But somehow, the powerful corona around him seems more diminished than before. You then realize what's happening. Mordo isn't making a move against you. The power around Doc is

22

diminishing—the power that Mordo is generating. Transporting you to Rome, London and Morocco, not to mention sending Doc's form out of the house, has taken its toll on Mordo. Even with the mystic strength of the quarter-amulet he possesses, he must be really drained.

You turn back to him and, indeed, he looks weak. But his face is still fierce and scowling, his voice has lost none of its power.

You glance at Clea, hoping for some guidance, but she's slumped in a corner, depleted of energy by the journey. Her face is whiter than her hair—clearly as a practitioner of the mystic arts, she's not in Mordo's or Strange's league.

You clutch the amulet as Mordo holds up the quarter-amulet he possesses. "Give it here, Spider-Man!" he shouts. "Give it to me and you can go on your way, free and unharmed. Fight me, and you'll die a hideous, lingering death!"

"Is there any other kind?" you ask, quickly trying to figure your next move. You're sure not going to give him the amulet. What other choices have you got?

You can try to snag the quarter-amulet from Mordo's hand, using your webbing (**210**), attack Mordo directly (**192**), or try to free Doc and let him mop up this mess (**24**).

After all, Mordo's his bad guy, not yours.

"Why?" you ask cagily. "Just who the **12** devil do you think I'm made out to be?"

He looks heavenward. "Save me from crazy Americans," he sighs. "It's quite obvious who you are—you're a rather demented young man on his way to a costume party. Only an American would

23

act in such an outlandish fashion. Certainly no proper Briton would. Be off with you, then." He turns and walks off, twirling his truncheon. A few paces away, he runs into a couple of other bobbies, and they all glance in your direction and laugh.

The heck with it, you think, turning and trotting down into the underground.

Give yourself 1 Karma point for your adroit handling of a potentially tricky situation, then go to **31**.

13   Summoning every ounce of determination and aggressiveness, you leap forward. You ignore the buffeting you're taking from the winds, ignore the shouts of Mordo to surrender before it's too late. Every muscle in your body is strained to the utmost as you hurtle forward, as if fired from a cannon.

Mordo only has time to shout an angry curse, before his jaw is greeted by your knuckles.

He topples back and you become absolutely relentless. This is your only shot and you can't risk screwing it up. You tear into Mordo, pounding as hard as you can. Mordo, who may be an absolute master of sorcery, is at a loss to put up any kind of physical defense, but you're not giving him the time to think.

That's the pure joy of depending on your fists. You don't have to think. You just swing at any target presented to you. He tries to fight off your punches as he blocks his head, and you smash him in the stomach, doubling him over. You then drive an uppercut to his bearded chin that lifts him off his feet. He lands on his back and you approach him, not wanting to.

He lifts his head and, his eyes crossing, lifts a hand and starts to say, "By the hoar—" He then slumps back, his head hitting the ground with a resounding thud.

"Hey!" you admonish him. "Watch your language, fella. There's a lady present." But you know that he no longer hears you.

You step over to Clea and shake her gently. "You okay?"

Slowly she opens her eyes. "Stephen—?"

"Spidey," you reply. You hand her the amulet. "Here. This thing gives me the whim-whams. Hold on to it while I web up mudball here."

You walk over to Mordo and, within moments, have cocooned him from head to toe in webbing, with extra sticky stuff on his mouth to keep it sealed shut. The last thing you need this guy to do is wake up and start mumbling some new spells.

Just before you web up his hands, you pry from his grasp the remaining quarter of the Caputo amulet. Turning to Clea, you say, "Here. This goes with that," and you toss her the remaining quarter.

Go to **113**.

Suddenly, you are surrounded by Doctor **14** Stranges. A dozen images, all identical, are closing in on you. You close your eyes, trying to depend on your spider-sense. But insanely, every one of these advancing images is setting off your spider-sense. You have no idea in which direction to turn, or who to go after.

"Not fair!" you shout, then abruptly feel a fist slam into you. As you are knocked backward you only have time to think to yourself, *Man, I never knew Doc Strange packed such a punch.*

You go down, slipping into unconsciousness (and losing 4 Health points—subtract them from your total).

If you're still among the living, go to **134**.

15 Summoning all your nerve, you leap toward the amulet. Make an Agility FEAT roll. If the result is 12 or less, go to **115**. If it's 13 or more, go to **125**.

16 You think to yourself, *That guy looks as if he could turn me into bubble gum with a wave of his hand—and I'm the only guy who knows about him. I've gotta tell somebody.*

You turn and start to crawl down the wall, away from the Sanctum. You're halfway down, when you suddenly hear an angry shout from the Sanctum, and the sounds of tremendous bursts of power being unleashed. Two voices speak now—the man's, and a woman's. They're both chanting spells as quickly as they can.

And then, before you can make a move, there's a huge burst of light followed by absolute silence.

Go to **61**.

17 What Clea didn't give you a chance to tell her—the piece that suddenly clicked into place for you—is that you're now convinced that Mordo is still back at the house.

You fire a webline and start swinging quickly across the city, back toward the Greenwich Village townhouse.

He has to be there, because none of this makes any sense if he's left. What he told you, while disguised as Doctor Strange, was based in truth. There had been a battle, all right, and it must have ended up at Doc's townhouse. There, a mystic spell was cast, all right, preventing one of them from leaving the house.

However, it was Doctor Strange who had cast the spell—a spell physically binding Mordo to the building. And even though Mordo had managed to encase Doc in that mystic barrier you saw earlier, Doc must still be conscious—and mentally keeping the spell in place, so that Mordo can't go running around trying to assemble the other pieces of the amulet (the locations of which Mordo obviously managed to pry from Strange's mind).

But Mordo was still able to send out his spirit form, and he managed to disguise that form so that you were suckered into thinking you were dealing with Doc Strange. He used the power of one-quarter of the amulet to shift you around from place to place while he himself was held prisoner by Doc's spell.

And where is Wong, Strange's manservant? Probably being held prisoner within the walls of the townhouse.

The thing is, there's no reason to assume that the original spell Strange placed on Mordo has diminished—the spell that forced Mordo to use you as a physical agent. If that's the case, then all Mordo did was transplant himself somewhere within that same house—and you simply assumed that he'd taken himself elsewhere.

Go to **117**.

18   You wait to see if something else is tossed at you, but nothing comes. Furthermore, the amulet symbol on the wall is no longer there.

Mystic spell must be like a battery charge, you think. *Eventually, it starts to wear off, has to be renewed. If it goes into action, it gets used up quicker, like now.*

You pull back a fist and smash it into the wall. You're simply in no mood for subtleties today.

The wall crumbles easily in front of you, and you reach in and feel around. You pray that your spider-sense will warn you if something inside decides to have your arm for a snack.

Your fingers close around a triangular piece of

28

stone which you realize immediately is the piece of amulet you're looking for.

You turn it over and over in your hand, trying to make sense of the markings on it. Oh well, the heck with it—you're a scientist and shutterbug, not an archaelogist.

You tuck the quarter-amulet into your belt and look up as Doc Strange's ectoplasmic spirit hovers in front of you.

"Gimme a sec," you say. "I need a few minutes to repair my equipment, get my stuff together." But instead of waiting, Doc merely waves his hand and, to your surprise, you suddenly feel robust and healthy. Add 4 points to your Health score (keeping in mind that you can't exceed 32). You test your web shooters, and they work perfectly.

"You're just what the doctor ordered, Doc," you say. But he merely floats in the air with his arms folded, waiting—not for praise, but for you to make some sort of decision.

If you want to go to Rome, go to **91**.

If you want to go to Morocco, go **119**.

If you don't have all the sections of the amulet, but want to call it quits, proceed to **181**.

If this was your last stop and you have the other sections of the amulet, go to **217**.

You close your eyes and gather strength. **19** You know that you have Mordo in your mind, but knowing gives you the strength you need to overcome. Once you know there's a fight, nothing can stop you from winning it. Absolutely nothing.

You stagger slightly and you hear Mordo say, "Spider-Man? What the—"

He never gets the rest of the sentence out. With blinding speed, you leap at him just as he picks up the amulet. He drops it, however, the instant your fist connects with his face.

Mordo is hurled back, blood pouring from his nose. He tries to pull himself together, tries to mount a defense—physical, mystic, anything—but it's too late, as, with one final roundhouse punch, you lay Mordo out.

From across the room, Doctor Strange says wanly, "Welcome back."

"Welcome back? Did I ever leave?" you ask.

"For a brief time there, we had some bad moments," Strange says evenly. "However, it's clear that you were able to overcome your—difficulties."

"Right. Not bad for a normal guy, eh, Clea?"

Doc turns to Clea and, as he helps her to her feet, she says, with a certain amount of good-natured sarcasm, "A man in a costume who can crawl walls and shoot webs? Why, Spider-Man, you're as normal as I am."

"Gee, thanks. That's real praise coming from the Empress of the Dark Dimension."

Go to **242**.

20 Make an Agility FEAT roll, adding Karma if you wish. If the result is 12 or less, go to **231**. If the result is 13 or more, go to **235**.

21 "All right," says Dagger. "All right—I'll help you."

From behind you, a voice thick with anger says, "Dagger! Are you mad?"

"The amulet quarter—where is it?" you ask anxiously.

"The top of the tower—"

"Dagger!" Cloak is furious, and as you turn your head to look up toward the top of the tower, Cloak lunges at you. Light daggers flash past your shoulder, barely more than a blur, and plunge into Cloak. He is stunned for a moment, ecstasy passing over his face, and you remember what a tortured individual he is. The darkness that fills him is like a hungry entity, and the only thing that can give him momentary relief is the living light that Dagger can produce.

It's an opportunity you can't waste. As Dagger hurls more bolts of light at him, locking him in his place, you bound past Cloak and head up the stairs. He shouts after you but it's a faint, distant effort, so distracted is he.

Go to **121**.

Your web shots miss, as Dagger, with the **22** skill and grace of a ballerina, leaps toward you and effortlessly avoids them. With an underhand motion, as if hurling a softball, she lets loose with two daggers. They slice through your body, numbing you. A chill cuts into your bones and you feel the energy sapped momentarily from your muscles. Subtract 5 Health points from your total.

Go to **212**.

"Look, Doc, I know you're really eager to **23** get it—but you and I have to talk."

Your spider-sense starts to go off as Strange's

31

smile loses all its warmth, if it ever had any to begin with. He steps down from his lotus position. You're not sure how, because there's no wind, or for that matter a window, in the room, but the master mage's cape begins blowing back behind him.

"Do not cross me, Spider-Man," he says angrily. "I am a valuable ally—and a deadly foe. Give me the amulet—*now*."

You back up. Something is terribly, terribly wrong with Doc, and you don't want to hang around to find out what it is. You glance around quickly, looking for a way out. As you noticed before, there are no windows, although you could have sworn earlier that there were. Could windows vanish in Doc's house? Why not? People do. And you just might end up as one of those people.

You back toward the door and it suddenly slams shut behind you. Tentatively, not taking an eye off the advancing magician, you push against it. It doesn't seem remotely interested in opening, and you realize that there is something more than a simple earthbound lock that is keeping it shut.

You glance to your left and see a stairway leading up and out of sight. And there's an extremely irate magician directly in front of you. The amulet throbs in your hand.

"Last warning, Spider-Man," says Strange, and his hands start to move in a way that you've come to recognize very quickly as preparing to cast a spell.

Do you try to somehow make use of the amulet (**105**), fire your webbing (**35**), or try to outmaneuver him (**230**)?

Without hesitation, you leap toward Doc, **24** covering the distance between you easily. You stand poised over the imprisoned master magician and, from across the room, Mordo shouts, "No! You don't know what you're doing! The amulet's already surging with power! If you add more to it, with your untrained mind—"

"Hey, come on, Mordy," you snap. "You can't possibly think I'm stupid enough to fall for a line like that. Well, it's not going to work, fella. Doc's breaking loose, right now, courtesy of your friendly neighborhood Spider-Man."

Go to **152**.

Your head stops spinning, and suddenly, a **25** roaring fills your ears. You look around in shock.

The Coliseum is no longer ancient and unkempt, with large chunks of fallen rock here and there. Instead it's new, as if built yesterday. The seats are filled with screaming skeletons, dressed in togas and similar ancient Roman garb.

And you're in the middle of the Coliseum, with a bad feeling about this.

One spectator's box is adorned with purple flags, and you can almost feel the power emanating from it.

Seated in the box is the man you intended to save moments ago—the Roman emperor.

You sure can pick 'em.

Go to **53**.

Make an Agility with Webbing FEAT roll. If **26** the result is 19 or more, go to **175**. If it's 18 or less, go to **126**.

Your web shot is right on the mark. Your **27** webbing covers Hobby's weapons bag as well as his midsection.

"You think to stop me with this puny weapon?!" he howls.

"Nah! I've got lots more puny weapons—like my spider-strength and—"

Suddenly, you hear a train approaching, and feel it, as well, as it rumbles toward you. Even as you realize the possibilities, you've checked to make sure your feet are solidly anchored to the floor. Nothing can make you unstick against your will. Bracing yourself, you put your strength to the test and swing the pseudo-Hobgoblin toward the path of the oncoming train.

Perform a Strength FEAT roll, adding Karma if you wish. If the result is 12 or less, go to **47**. If the result is 13 or more, go to **71**.

Slowly, the world comes back into focus. **28**

You start to sit up, your mind clearing, feeling as if someone had rammed a pike through your skull. You slump back, moaning.

Doctor Strange stands over you, passing his hands over your face. "Is that—some sort of spell, Doc?"

"Ah!" says Doctor Strange. "You're awake. It's difficult to tell with someone wearing a full face mask."

"Yeah, I'm awake, though I've got the world's biggest headache."

Doc stands up and says, "Take two of the world's biggest aspirin and call me in the morning."

"Whoa! Doc Strange makes a funny."

From nearby, you hear Clea say, "Stephen has always had a sense of humor. He simply chooses to display his at appropriate times."

"Now, Clea," says Doc. "Spider-Man has been through a great deal. There is no need to belabor it."

"Where's Mordo," you ask, slowly standing. "Where's the amulet?"

"Both disposed of."

"And me? How'd I wind up—?"

"I'm afraid the amulet managed to take over your psyche. Fortunately, we were dealing with only the partial amulet, and I was able to overcome it. Otherwise, it could have been very, very unpleasant."

"It took me over—just like that." You shake your head in disgust.

Doc puts a hand on your shoulder. "Do not be so

hard on yourself, my friend," he says. "The Caputo amulet is a powerful mystic tool. It's understandable that you would submit to its influence."

"It's not understandable to me," you say angrily. "It sold me a bill of goods and I bought it. I should've been able to fight it off—not have to depend on you to save my hash."

Without another word, you turn and walk out of Doc's Greenwich Village home. You pause outside, breathing the evening air.

You had a near miss, and you really owe Doc a lot. On the other hand, he really owes you, too. It's a wash, you guess. But it still leaves a bad taste in your mouth.

Aiming a webline, you swing up and out into the city.

You flip nimbly out of the way, putting **29** your hands up in front of your face to ward off flying fragments of pumpkin grenade. Several slam into your wrists but you don't sustain any health damage, luckily, as you land on your feet.

Go to **5**.

You follow the trail of smoke now, five **30** more blocks, and then you see it. A three-story brick building, flames billowing out of the windows, the breeze fanning them and bringing them higher.

You pause on the roof opposite the burning building. And you hear someone screaming.

Flame isn't coming out of all the windows. Through one window you can see a woman, trapped on the third floor, waving her arms frantically. Her situation is desperate, but not hopeless. The first and second floors are in bad shape, but the third is not completely consumed. Unfortunately, the firemen aren't here yet. Fortunately, you are. And so is a golden opportunity for news photos.

It'll only take you a few seconds to set up your camera. If you pause to do so, swing over to **63**. If you choose to go directly to save the woman, go to **140**.

31 Once inside the stairwell, you find quite a crowd on the escalator going down. People are standing to the right and dashing past on the left, but you want a bit more speed either way. You hop onto the wall and skitter down, bypassing the escalator altogether and garnering quite a few surprised looks from the train riders.

You get down to the platform just as a train is pulling out. You marvel at how clean and slick it looks, especially compared with New York trains. *Of course, anything's better than New York subways*, you think, hopping on top, and clinging to it with your adhering power.

Turn to **41**.

32 The Coliseum is a huge, round arena, the middle now decayed, revealing the maze of passageways below. You crawl along the perimeter wall toward the shouting, which continues unabated. You glance back toward the middle but Doc is now gone—probably having trouble with that containment spell.

At last you get there, calling, "Have no fear!

38

Your friendly roamin' Roman Spider-Man is here."

Peering into the seats, you see a man lying there, tied up and helpless. Wary of a trick, you look him over, but don't recognize him as any of your old foes, imagined or otherwise. He looks angry as all get out, and he shouts, "Well?! Don't crouch there looking spidery—get me out of this."

The only problem is, your spider-sense is going crazy—but you're not sure why.

If you want to untie him (after all, he's just one unarmed guy) go to **42**. If you decide to back off (and feel like a world-class heel), go to **57**.

Putting your full strength into it, you grab **33** the Rhino and hoist him over your head.

"Alley oop, ugly!" you shout as the Rhino helplessly flails his arms and legs. With one more powerful burst of energy, you hurl the Rhino up and at the emperor.

The centurions see him coming and this time, rather than readying their lances, they bolt. A costumed webbed wonder is one thing—but this is 500 pounds of hurled Rhino, and they don't want anything to do with him.

A roar goes up around you and you hear a shriek mixed in with it—from the emperor.

The emperor throws up his arms as if to ward off the Rhino, but there's no way. The Rhino lands on top of him, and the emperor's scream is cut off by a crunching of bones.

There is an explosion, and the sound of air "whooshing" in as if to fill a vacuum.

You hold your ground, bracing yourself against it, and the world seems to collapse around you. The Coliseum seems to have aged massively almost in an instant, and then you realize that you're back where you were before.

All the people are gone. The Rhino, the emperor, Mary Jane. Everyone.

One easy leap carries you into the emperor's box and there, in the ancient stones, is the fading symbol of the amulet.

Somehow, the quarter-amulet's power had taken on an actual personification of the emperor, you decide. When you destroyed the emperor, just as you'd hoped, you destroyed the amulet's resistance.

Give yourself 2 Karma points for overcoming these bizarre odds, and go to **43**.

34 "Look—I'm sorry, Kathy, but something's come up. I can't take the assignment," you tell her. "I have to—"

"I don't care what you have to do, Parker," she tells you sharply. "You're on shakey enough ground as it is. And now you're turning down assignments? What's the matter, need some time off? Been 'not working' too hard?"

"It's not like that. It's—"

"No, forget it, Parker. I'll give it to Bannon. I can count on him, at least." She stalks off.

Great, you think to yourself. For a while there you'd thought that Lance Bannon was actually your arch enemy, the Hobgoblin. You've since learned otherwise, which is a shame, because it would have been the perfect excuse to punch his lights out. Ah, well.

Maybe Cushing is steamed, but at least you can console yourself with 1 Karma point for being conscientious.

You head up to the roof, and moments later are swinging toward Doctor Strange's Greenwich Village digs.

Go to **80**.

"Now hold on, Doc—let's talk this over," **35** you say, quickly bringing your webshooters up and firing. It's an utterly useless gesture, as Doc effortlessly deflects the web spray with a mystic shield. "Wow," you say, trying to buy some time. "Can you teach me to do that?"

Doc spreads his hands wide, and bolts of magical energy leap from them. You hesitate, unsure of which way to go or what to do.

"I'm warning you, Spider-Man!" he calls to you. "The amulet is a device of unlimited mystic potential. The longer you hold it, the greater the danger you put us all in. End this foolishness and hand me the amulet before it's too late. Otherwise the power could destroy you—destroy all of us!"

Do you do as he suggests and give up the amulet (**163**), or hold on to it and back away (**173**)?

You leap into the air, glancing back to apol- **36** ogize for the mess you've made of things. At that moment, your spider-sense warns you, but too late. A thrown truncheon blindsides you and you hit the ground, sustaining 2 points of health damage.

Make an Endurance FEAT roll. If the result is 10 or less, go to **161**. If it is 11 or more, go to **46**.

37   You feel the full, proportionate strength of a spider coursing through you, as you leap clear of the oncoming train. The Hobgoblin hesitates a moment to shout of what he's going to do to you, then the train smashes into him, returning him to the mystic dust from which he came.

Go to **18**.

38   You make it to the top of the stairs and don't even hesitate at the door barring your way. You kick it open and stop, shocked at what you see.

But he's *behind* you! You can tell by the howls of fury and the curses. "Doc," you whisper.

The master mage is bereft of his cloak and his amulet. He floats there in some sort of stasis field. He stares up, unseeing, at the ceiling, his body paralyzed, his breathing non-existent.

Is he dead? is your first horrified thought.

You glance around and realize that you're in his Sanctum Sanctorum, the stronghold where his power is normally at its strongest. If something were actually able to overcome him here, in his place of power, then it would have to be one of his most formidable foes.

But you look at the throbbing piece of rock in your hand and think to yourself, *Hey. At this second, I'm pretty formidable myself. Whatever this thing is, it clearly has the power to absorb spells and mystic energy.* And the faintly glowing aura around Doc is most certainly that.

You leap forward, ready to slam the amulet into it and release Doc. But an instant before you come into contact with him, he vanishes. You stand there, helpless and frustrated.

Go to **48**.

She tries to dart out of your way, her lips **39** moving to utter a spell. But one webshot from you covers her mouth before she can summon Dormammu, or any of those other fun guys you heard being mentioned. Another webshot encompasses her body and she spins, out of control, sinking momentarily from sight.

For someone with mystic abilities, it's unlikely that she'll be held long by your webbing. It's a good time for you to get the heck out of here.

Go to **207**.

You land with a thud and abruptly feel a **40** chill wind cutting through you. Snow whirls around you, and hits you with the impact of a sledgehammer and you wither, but do not wilt under the onslaught. For all the protection your costume affords, you might as well be wearing Bermuda shorts and a T-shirt.

All around you, mountains stretch upward as high as you can see. Then, you realize, if *your* costume isn't protecting *you* from the hideous climate around you, Clea must be in even worse shape. Then again, maybe she can whip up some sort of mystic shield to protect herself.

You turn, and see her several yards away. Again, however, she looks wan and drawn, and the amulet is glowing even more brightly. That thing is definitely starting to give you the creeps.

Then, several hundred yards away, you see a glowing, unmoving form. The wind howls around you, making it almost impossible to even hear yourself think, much less talk with someone. "Clea, where the heck are we?!"

"I think," she starts to say, wavering in place, "I

think this is the area Stephen calls—the Himalayas!"

"Aw, wonderful!" The chill is beginning to work it's way deep into your body. You point off in the direction of the glow and shout, "I think I see Doc over there!"

"Yes," she says nodding. Her hair is already becoming stiff with frost, her face chapped. "Yes, we have to—" Suddenly a huge gust of wind knocks her flat on her back. The amulet flies from her fingers, landing several feet away. The snow around the amulet starts melting.

She starts to stagger to her feet—and your spider-sense goes wild.

"Clea!" you shout. "There's danger!"

"What?!" she calls back, managing to half-stand up. "What did you—"

Her question is broken by an ear-splitting roar. Go to **157**.

41 After riding for several minutes, you spot a glowing ball of energy on your left. It looks kind of like Tinkerbell as it hovers for a moment then floats off.

Must be from Doc, you think. *Guy would make a great compass.* You leap off the train, landing on another set of tracks leading in the opposite direction.

Beyond the tracks, the floating globe of light hovers, waiting for you to follow it. You do so, because what are your options?

The ball leads you about ten yards to the side and hovers a moment in front of a section of the tiled wall, then vanishes. Halfway up the wall is a symbol—a disk, split into four quarters—glowing slightly.

I know what that means, you think, reaching for the wall. Behind it, you're certain, is one-quarter of the amulet.

All of a sudden, your spider-sense goes haywire, and you're just as certain that, once again, you're in deep.

Materializing in front of you, as big as life and twice as ugly, is the Hobgoblin. The cowled, cackling villain floats on his goblin glider, blocking your way.

"You've come a long way, Spider-Man, to meet your death!" he says laughing.

He's not the real article, you tell yourself. *He's just plucked from my memories. But he can kill me just as dead.*

That, it is clear, is exactly his intention, as he reaches into the weapons bag slung over his shoulder.

You have two options: use your webbing (**51**), or leap directly at him and engage him in battle (**56**).

You leap forward, reach down and snap **42** the bonds keeping the man's hands together. He reaches up, grabs you by the forearm and suddenly the world goes haywire. You feel like you're going three rounds with a dryer spin cycle.

Go to **25**.

Clenching your fist, you smash through **43** the stone bench and within seconds, you have your fingers around the stone fragment that is a quarter of the amulet. This one feels warm to your grasp, almost pulsing.

Something real strange is going on, you think.

Right on cue, Doctor Strange's spirit materializes in front of you, arms folded.

"Not much for small talk, are you, Doc?" You ask. His eyes widen as you stick the quarter-amulet in your belt.

The next move is yours. If you want to go to London, go to **111**. If your destination is Morocco, then **119**. If you want to call it quits, go to **181**. If you've got all three pieces, then go to **217**.

44 *Something's weird here,* you think to yourself. *Aw, the heck with it. Everything about Doc Strange is weird. If he were normal, he'd call himself Doctor Normal.*

Go to **100**.

The Hulk abruptly leaps at you, an animal **45** growl escaping from his throat.

Make an Agility FEAT roll. If the result is 13 or less, go to **96**. If it is 14 or more, go to **55**.

The bobbies converge on you, but you ef- **46** fortlessly knock them aside, while saying, "The day I can't handle a bunch of guys named Bobby is the day I hang up my webs." By the same token, you have the uncomfortable feeling that that day came a lot closer than you intended.

Shoving the last of the embattled Britons aside, you leap into the entrance of the underground.

Go to **31**.

You hold on tight to your webbing, but be- **47** fore you can fully bring your strength to bear, the Hobgoblin kicks his glider into high gear. It pulls you forward and rips you from the ground, pieces of the floor adhering to your feet.

He swings you around like he's snapping a whip. You fall into the train track, and there's a brief glimmer of blinding white light.

Go to **196**.

"You young fool," an angry voice says. **48**

You turn to see Doc standing there. With a cutting edge in your tone, you say, "Still keeping up the disguise? Who are you, anyway?"

"I am," he says menacingly, "the last person you will see in this lifetime." The mage raises his hands and you know that he's about to cut loose at you with everything he's got. "Give me the amulet!" he shouts. "You are like a child with a loaded weapon. You have no idea what could happen to you!"

Do you stay and fight him, in hopes of discovering where he's sent Doc (**58**), or get out while the getting's good (**68**)?

49   You might as well give it a shot, although you're not exactly Mister Wizard.

You swing around the city, looking for someplace quiet where you can concentrate. That's more difficult than it sounds, when you're talking about New York City—everywhere you go, there seems to be construction or ambulances wailing or children screaming or police sirens howling.

Eventually, however, you wind up on top of Saint Patrick's Cathedral. People below you go about their business, and no one seems to notice you. Which is just fine by you.

You hold the amulet in your hands and concentrate, feeling a warmth beginning to fill you.

And the amulet seems to whisper to you, *What would you like?*

Good lord, you think. *I'm actually communicating with it.*

You pull your somewhat scattered wits together and think, *Bring me to Doctor Strange.*

You have not the skill, it replies.

Angrily, you reply *What do I need to do it?*

Training in the mystic arts, the voice replies. *Either that—or my fourth part.*

If I had the fourth part, you think, *I'd probably be where Doctor Strange is.*

Ah, it says, sounding so convincing, *but if you*

had the fourth part, I could give you power. In-
credible power. And I know that you could use
this power responsibly, for it's part of your nature.

Yes, you think. *Tell me how. Tell me—*

Someone is listening, it suddenly says, and immediately you feel a void. The voice in your head
is gone.

The amulet grows cooler in your hand and you
shake it angrily. "Wait a minute!" you snap.
"Don't cut out on me. What do you—" But nothing you say or do coaxes the amulet to speak any
further.

Go to **207**.

The fire chief is standing there. "Glad you **50**
could make it," you say, even as firemen are running around you, spraying water into the fire.

"Don't get flip with me," says the fire chief. "Of-
ficially, I have to say that that was the most brain-
less stunt I've ever seen."

"And unofficially?"

The chief actually half-smiles but then forces it
away. "No comment," he says.

Go to **60**.

Make an Agility with Webbing FEAT roll, **51**
adding Karma if you wish. If the result is 19 or
less, go to **74**. If the result is 20 or more, go to **27**.

You work your way toward the center of **52**
the Coliseum, moving carefully. Suddenly, you realize that your perspective was off—Doc was not
floating over the dead center of the arena. He was

off toward the far end. He was so high up in the air that you didn't realize it. Now, though, he's definitely at one end, pointing downward. He hangs there a moment or two more, then vanishes.

"Not making this easy, are you, Doc?" you think to yourself ruefully.

Suddenly, the ground under you starts to shake. You look around frantically even as your spider-sense buzzes in alarm. Something's heading your way. Something big. What have the mystic defenses cooked up this time? You get the sneaking suspicion that you don't want to know.

Go to **79**.

You look to the far end of the arena. There **53** you see a woman tied to a large stake. Her head is slumped forward, her face hidden by cascading red hair. She looks up, and her chapped lips mutter one word: "Peter."

In shock, you gasp, "Mary Jane!"

She's fifty yards away and you automatically take a step toward her before hesitating. Is it another trap?

At the end of the arena opposite MJ, a large, grated door slides upward.

"I don't believe any of this!" you shout, certain that what you're witnessing must be a hallucination.

Then, from the entrance uncovered by the rising gate, a massive grey form charges out. If it weren't striding on two legs you'd think it was some sort of animal, especially with the huge horn on the front of its head.

But it's not an animal, and even as the ground beneath you shakes under his tread, you recognize him instantly.

The Rhino! And he's charging straight toward Mary Jane!

Go to **72**.

54   "I'm Spider-Man," you say. "I'm in the middle of trying to save the world from going up in flames. That do it for you?"

"Oh, it certainly does, my lad." He reaches to take you by the wrist. "You're crazy as a loon. Better come with me."

This is another of the countless times that cops are getting in your way when you're trying to do something important. No one else has to put up with this kind of treatment.

"Look, you obviously need some convincing to stay out of my way," you snap. You grab the stunned bobby by the front of his coat and lift him clear off his feet with one hand. "This do it for you?"

Even as you speak you mentally kick yourself for blowing your temper. Reduce your Karma total by 1 point for handling the situation with chain mail gloves rather than kid ones.

Immediately, you set the bobby on his feet, but it's too late for the apologies you try to make. He shoves a whistle in his mouth and starts to blow.

"Now just a min—" you start, but then you see half a dozen bobbies charging toward you, all waving their truncheons. You feel like you're trapped in a Keystone Cops comedy, but you're not laughing.

Your best move is to get out of here. Make an Agility FEAT roll, adding Karma if you want to put more spring in your step. If the result is 12 or less, go to **36**. If it's 13 or more, go to **64**.

As the Hulk comes down, you go up, leap- **55** ing high in the air as he thuds to the ground with an earth-shattering crash. Even as he lands, you spin in mid-air and, hitting the Hulk's back with both feet, launch yourself through the air as if you were a swimmer kicking off from the pool wall.

"Hey!" shouts the Hulk, grabbing for you. But you've already taken off like a rocket.

Go to **65**.

Adding Karma if you wish, make an Agili- **56** ty FEAT roll. If the result is 14 or less, go to **66**. If it's 15 or more, go to **76**.

You don't like the looks of this at all. **57** *What's this guy doing here? Why is it that the tour group that was through here just minutes ago didn't notice him?*

You back off and he stares at you, shouting angrily, "Let me loose from here, you wall-crawling coward. Let me go or I'll—I'll get really angry."

You pause, impressed by the histrionics, and then you fire a webline at him.

He vanishes as the webline goes right through him.

Some sort of trap, obviously. Erected by the mystic defenses that the quarter-amulet has to offer. You wonder just what would have happened if you'd gotten within range of that pseudo-guy, and you decide that you're happy you didn't find out.

Give yourself 1 Karma point for your cleverness.

Go to **52**.

58   Holding the amulet out in front of you, you shout, "Yeah, well, the thing about loaded guns is that they go off at the people they're aimed at. So let's see how you do when this child throws a tantrum!"

He blanches as you charge him full-steam, your fist pulled back. If the amulet absorbs his mystic attacks, that means it's going to be a man-to-man fight. And in a purely physical encounter, there's no doubt in your mind who the victor will be.

Apparently, there's no doubt in his mind either. He vanishes before you can connect with a blow. Add 2 Karma points to your total for your aggressive, gutsy handling of the situation.

You have only seconds to savor your "victory," as his voice fills the air. "You've won this battle, Spider-Man. But my demons will be after you. You'll have no respite, nowhere to hide. Eventually the Caputo amulet will be mine, and the world as well!"

You comb your mind for a clever response.

"Oh, yeah?" you shout, realizing that your retort seems to fall just a little flat. With a sigh, you glance up at the window with the elaborate curved design you've seen before—the skylight that leads outside.

As good a way as any of exiting, you think to yourself. You climb up to the window, push it open, and swing out into the city.

Go to **207**.

The important thing is to try to lure her **59** away from your apartment. If something big went down, you'd be much too close to your place to be remotely comfortable.

And as you start to bolt, she calls after you, "Stephen Strange sent me."

You pause and turn, still leery of listening to her. You're ready to move if she should make the slightest move against you.

"He called out to me," she said. "He managed to briefly break through some sort of spell that was entrapping him. He needs my help, and he needs yours. He told me to find you."

She takes a step toward you in the air, and you back away. Slightly annoyed, she purses her lips and places her hands on her hips.

"Listen to me," she says, trying to sound reasonable. "If you fight me, I won't fight back, which means you'll be pummeling a woman who won't lift a hand in defense. If you try to run," and she inclines her head in the direction of your apartment, "I can go after the young woman who's in that apartment if I wish. If I'm evil, as you clearly fear, then it's certain death for her. If I'm on your side, however, as I say—then you'd want to listen to me. So what will it be?"

You stand there, considering what she's saying. "All right," you finally say, "I'll listen."

Go to **110**.

60 The police help the recently saved and somewhat confused, hysterical woman into a squad car. She's shaken and babbling something that sounds almost incoherent. If you hurry, you can get back up to the roof where you left your camera, squeeze off a couple of shots and get over to the *Bugle* before deadline. On the other hand, maybe you want to give a listen to what she's saying—although to do so could blow the deadline for the evening edition. If you want to risk wasting your time with her, go to **70**. If you want to go straight to the *Bugle*, go to **104**.

61 You head back up to the Sanctum at full speed, but by the time you get there it's empty. Doc's floating body is gone, as is the Doc Strange impersonator. As near as you can tell, the mysterious female you heard is also gone.

The air still crackles with the energies released. Something happened here, something big. Whoever the female was who turned up just now, she obviously tried to save Doc. Or maybe she was just power hungry and wanted that stupid amulet for herself. Either way, it's out of your hands now.

You hope, however, that when it gets sorted out, the good guys win this one.

"No way!" you shout, snapping free. Sud- **62** denly, your mind is clear—you realize that you came within a hairbreadth of falling completely under the spell of this insidious amulet.

You hurl it aside, and it bounces against a corner of the room and sits there, glowing malevolently.

On the opposite side of the room, Mordo shouts, "Mine! It must be mine!" He takes a step toward the amulet, but gets no farther. Crimson bars of energy appear around him, barring his way. He slams his hands against them, furious.

You turn to see Doc Strange standing there. This time he looks as you're accustomed to seeing him—confident, stoic.

He turns to you and says, "That should take care of Mordo. Are you all right, Spider-Man? You look shaken."

"Shaken, but not stirred," you manage to say.

"Consider yourself fortunate that you did not have the complete Caputo amulet to deal with," he says. "The power of *that* would have been such that—" Suddenly his eyes widen. "Clea!"

You don't even see him move. One moment he's next to you, the next moment he's cradling Clea's head in his lap. Her eyes flutter open, and the look exchanged between the two of them confirms the depth of feeling that, until now, you've only just surmised.

"Clea," he says. "You got my message."

"It would be—difficult," she says through chapped lips, "to ignore a summons from the sorceror supreme. Fortunately," and she glances toward you, "I had a staunch ally at my side."

"It was nothing," you say. "Whenever I send my costume out to be cleaned, I always have them put extra staunch in it."

Go to **242**.

63   It'll only take you a couple of seconds to set up your camera and its automatic timer. Just a few seconds . . .

But seconds, it turns out, you don't have. The woman in the window suddenly screams and, even from across the street, you hear the crashing. She vanishes from the window and is replaced by billowing smoke. The ceiling, or a portion of it, must have collapsed.

Alarmed, you drop your camera and swing madly over to the building. Heedless of danger, your spider-sense screaming, you leap through the window, taking in big gulps of air.

You look around frantically, trying to locate the woman. You see a large burning beam nearby—that must be what fell. You're in an office, with a door to your left leading to what is probably an adjoining office. Smoke is all around, and your spider-sense is confused.

Make an Intuition FEAT roll. If the result is 13 or less, go to **85**. If it is 14 or more, go to **73**.

Gathering your spider-strength, you leap **64**
over the heads of the onrushing cops. Not only do
you clear them by several feet, but you easily
avoid several hurled truncheons. It's like fighting
an army of Daredevils.

They stand there for a moment, gaping, and
you take advantage of their momentary surprise
to bolt down into the subway station. "I can't
believe it! The blighter really *was* Spider-Man!"
you hear one of them say in shock. "Who
would've thought?"

Yeah, you think to yourself, *from the bonehead-
ed way I just acted, you'd think I was Moe, Curly,
and Larry all rolled into one.*

Go to **31**.

Your leap off the Hulk's back carries you **65**
up to the place where you think the amulet must
be hidden. And sure enough, there it is—or at
least the symbol that marks where it must be. It's
a circle, divided into quarters and glowing there
on the stone. Behind it, you're certain, is the piece
of the amulet you've come for.

At that moment, there's a tremendous crash.
The Hulk, in one easy leap, has landed next to
you.

"Cute trick," rumbles the Hulk. "Let's see you
try one now."

He lunges toward you, faster than you would
have given him credit for. His blockbuster arms
are on either side of you. There's only one option
open to you.

Make a Strength FEAT roll, adding Karma if you
wish. If the result is 13 or less, go to **107**. If it is 14
or more, go to **75**.

66   You leap forward, but the Hobgoblin puts on an extra burst of speed, jetting out of your way and delivering a paralyzing blow to the back of your neck. You land, quickly shaking off its effects, but not the 3 points of health damage you sustain.

Hobby swings around, peppering the ground at your feet with finger-blasts.

Go to **76**.

67   You try leaping out of the way, but the Rhino puts on an unexpected burst of speed and clips your leg in midair. You are hurled backward, the sky spinning around you and you hit the ground with a bone-crunching jar.

Reduce your Health score by 5 points. If the total reaches 0, you're history.

Otherwise, go to **77**.

68   *He's right,* you think desperately, *this thing could blow up in my face if I try to use it again.*

And out loud, you say, "You're right, guy. But I'll be back, and I'll find out what happened to Doc. And you, fella, are gonna regret every crummy thing you put me through."

You leap up effortlessly toward the great skylight with the cross-hatching design you've seen and admired so many times, then smash through it, swinging out into the evening air.

"You'll get no respite, wall-crawler!" he shouts after you. "My demons will hunt you down wherever you hide. You're finished, Spider-Man!"

Go to **78**.

You fire your webbing at what seems to be **69** point-blank range but, with unbelievable swiftness, she darts over it, skipping toward you.

I gotta get the heck out of here, you think.

Go to **59**.

What the heck. A couple more seconds **70** can't hurt, so you let yourself eavesdrop.

"It—it was incredible!" She's trying to convince the police. "I—I was coming out of my office and saw these two—two men, fighting. They were waving their hands, and bright light was coming out of their fingertips and—"

"Okay, miss," one of the cops is saying soothingly. "Let's get you to the hospital—"

"You've got to believe me!" She grabs at his shirt. "One of them—he had a red cape and was shouting something about the hairy hosts of hogwash. And the other guy was dressed in green—"

"Absolutely," says a cop. "Now get in the car. You may have inhaled some smoke and we want to get you to the hospital." Grudgingly, she gets in the back seat. The first cop glances at his partner and whistles the tune to "Twilight Zone."

But what she said already rings bells with you. There's only one guy who could match her description—Doctor Strange. You remember one of his snappy catch phrases, namely, "By the hoary hosts of Hoggoth." You never quite knew who Hoggoth was, or why his hosts were hoary, but that doesn't matter.

Add 1 Karma point for your time-saving decision to head straight to Doc's Greenwich Village abode.

Turn to **80**.

61

71   As the train roars within range, you put your back into it and, keeping a firm grip on the web line, swing the Hobgoblin around as if he were a yo-yo.

Not for a moment would you attempt such a deadly feat against a living foe. *But then, this is no living foe,* you reassure yourself, as the Hobgoblin falls right into the path of the train. It crashes into him, smashing him into a thousand small pieces that immediately crumble into dust and blow down the corridor.

You sag against the wall, letting out a sigh.

Go to **18**.

72   You leap toward the Rhino, shouting, "Hey horn-beak! You ever think of investing in a good pair of tennis shoes?"

"Spider-Man!" he grunts in a voice like a creaky hinge, and immediately he angles off toward you, at full-steam!

The crowd's roar fills your head and you see the emperor reclining on his stone seat and laughing hysterically.

Seconds ago there had been no one here—now it is packed with ancient Romans. Could the quarter of the amulet be powerful enough to summon spirits from another time, or to project you back? Or is it all an illusion, as you hope?

If it is, then the Rhino, who is now merely feet away, shouldn't be able to hurt you. Your spider-sense is tingling, but that could be from the influence of the amulet.

Do you want to stand your ground, testing your illusion theory (**225**), or play it safe and dodge the Rhino (**82**).

You sort out the conflicting warnings and **73**
look up just in time to see the ceiling collapsing.

Make an Agility FEAT roll. If the result is 12 or
less, go to **95**. If it is 13 or more, go to **83**.

You fire your webbing, figuring you've got **74**
him iced, but the pseudo-Hobgoblin puts on a
burst of speed with his glider that you weren't anticipating. He shoots just past your weblines,
pulls out his pumpkin bombs, and hurls them.

Make an Agility FEAT roll. If the result is 13 or
less, go to **84**. If it's 14 or more, go to **29**.

The Hulk is slightly off balance as he goes **75**
for you, and you use the moment to strike. Gathering up every ounce of strength in your spider-
powered muscles, you slam the Hulk in the jaw.

On the green Hulk, this would only result in
broken fingers. But on the smaller gray Hulk, it
staggers him, knocking him back.

The problem is that this move has also infuriated him. You've got about five seconds to act.

It should, however, be enough. You smash your
fist into the stone and it gives easily, as you hoped
it would. The Hulk roars behind you as you yank
out the missing quarter-amulet.

You swing your arm around, holding the piece
in front of you as the Hulk leaps. There's no dodg-
ing him this time, but it doesn't matter. The amulet quarter seems to respond to your grasp and
the Hulk passes right through you, his body rapidly becoming intangible.

"You web-slinging fink!" shouts the Hulk, and
then he vanishes.

The stone fragment pulses warmly in your fingers. Looking up, you see Doc Strange's spirit form in front of you, its arms folded.

"Hey, no problem," you tell Doc. "I always love going a couple of rounds with the Hulk." You stick the amulet quarter in your belt.

The next move is yours. If you want to go to London, go to **111**. If your destination is Morocco, then **119**. If you've had it with this mystic stuff, go to **181**. If you've got all three pieces, go to **217**.

76   He hovers there, a beautifully tempting target, as you leap at him and knock him back. He pinwheels toward the track and you pursue him. Before he can recover, you smash him in the face again, knocking him off his glider and onto the train track.

He staggers to his feet, shaking off the effects of your punch, and you start toward him when the ground starts to shake. Because of the battering you've taken, you're not sure what it is. Earthquake maybe? Or maybe the Hobgoblin's causing it with some sort of mystic backup from the amulet.

Your spider-sense is screaming now, and the Hobgoblin is on his feet as the rumbling grows stronger. Do you leap away from him (**86**), or press the attack (**202**)?

77   The crowd all around you is screaming for your blood. You almost wish you could give it to them. Because it's radioactive, it'd probably have the entire joint glowing.

You move faster and faster, strength building up

in your injured leg with every step.

"Lie down and die, Spider-Man!" shouts the Rhino, trying to draw a bead on you with his piggish eyes so that he can start another charge.

"Can't right now," you reply. "Have to wait for my coffee break. So tell me, Rhiney—what's it like looking like a 'before' picture for a health spa?"

Furious, the Rhino charges at you. This time, however, you have plenty of room to maneuver.

Go to **92**.

You swing frantically across the city, the **78** sun slowly setting, your mind racing even faster than your body. You've been tricked, royally snookered. How could you have been such a tremendous sap? Someone managed to defeat Doc Strange, take his place in his home and snookered you into getting all the pieces of this amulet needed to bring it to full strength.

Well, almost full strength. You've got three-quarters of the amulet and your mysterious opponent only has one-quarter of it. You land on a rooftop and examine one of the shards, turning it over and over in your hands.

"Where's the 'on' switch?" you wonder out loud. There must be some way of activating it, but you're no magician. You're just a somewhat confused part-time photographer and super-powered adventurer. This is *way* out of your league.

The amulet merely throbs warmly in your hands. It could care less about the frantic mental state you're in right now. You hold it in front of you, and it seems to glow. Seems to, heck. It's definitely glowing, and you can almost hear a

small voice in your mind.

It's saying, *Don't worry. I'll take care of you. I'll help you see where all your enemies are.*

Your mouth moves soundlessly. You don't believe it. This is a lousy piece of rock. How can it be chatting with you?

Look, says the little voice. *Look over there. I'll help you see something you wouldn't have seen before. Something that your untrained eyes would never have given you the skill to spot.*

You're so distracted by the voice that you almost forget to listen to that other perpetual voice, your spider-sense, which is telling you that ducking down right now would be an extremely good idea.

You drop down to the roof, peering out over the edge and, to your shock, you see ghosts floating across Manhattan. There are three of them, their heads wrapped in some sort of bandages or coverings. One is in the lead, pointing to the left and right, clearly issuing instructions to the other two. They nod in understanding and fly off in their respective courses.

Go to **88**.

A wall in front of you splinters and cracks, **79** and a huge gray fist smashes through. Then a second fist, and with a heart-rending crack, a massive gray form bursts into the arena. You gasp in shock as you recognize him.

"The Hulk!"

He steps forward, massive arms flexing, muscles like rolls of coiled wire glinting in the sun.

Once, the Hulk had been green and stupid, wanting only to be left alone. This, however, is the gray Hulk, whom you've met only once. Brutish, cunning and . . .

"Okay, web-spinner," he shouts. "Get over here so I can mash you into the ground. And hurry up! I'm a busy guy."

. . . *and a smart aleck,* you complete the thought.

You're standing twenty-five feet away from him—no distance for you to cover, if you are so inclined. Then again, not much trouble for him, either.

You don't even bother using your webbing. He'd snap it as if it were tissue paper.

Go to **45**.

80 Everytime you've had dealings with Doctor Strange, it's given you the whim-whams. The guy always seems to know far more about what's going on than he cares to tell you—and somehow, you never manage to muster the nerve to ask him more. Somehow, you don't *want* to know.

Within minutes, you've swung over to Doctor Strange's Greenwich Village digs. You pause outside this weird townhouse of his. There's that window in the roof with the bizarre crosshatching. The whole house makes your spider-sense tingle vaguely, and you're not sure why.

Your former girlfriend, the Black Cat, once told you how she tried to break into Strange's house. She jimmied a second story window, walked across the hall, opened a door and found herself standing outside on street level—and the door vanished behind her.

Fortunately, you're not the breaking-in type. You drop down to street level and knock on the front door. You anticipate that Strange's bald manservant, Wong, will answer the door as always, and you brush up on your bald jokes.

But, to your astonishment, the door swings open and it is the moustached magician himself, Doctor Strange, who is standing before you.

Make a combined Psyche and Intuition FEAT roll. If the result is 23 or less, go to **44**. If the result is 24, go to **90**.

"Nice—try, Seymour," you mutter, stag- **81** gering to your feet. "But it takes more than that to put your friendly neighborhood Spider-Man down for the count." *Not a whole lot more,* you add privately to yourself, though.

Seymour stands there a moment, crouched mere feet away from you. He then lifts his head back and roars a hideous animal scream.

You remember that one of the reasons animals roar is to momentarily paralyze their intended prey, which will presumably be so petrified that they will forget to run.

But Seymour doesn't have to do anything to freeze you. You already have lost all feeling in your toes. If you'd only known you were going to be making a hop to the Himalayas, you would have packed your spectacular spider-woolies.

Seymour rushes at you, waving his arms around like a great white, furry helicopter. You leap between his outstretched arms, flipping over his head, grabbing the monster's great shaggy head from the back, and putting him into a hammerlock.

Straining every muscle, you try to push the creature's head forward, while, at the same time, keep one powerful arm locked around his throat to cut off his air—to push him into unconsciousness. The difficulty is that you may be so depleted yourself, you may be unable to keep up the pressure.

Make a combined Strength and Endurance FEAT roll. If the result is 19 or less, go to **228**. If the result is 20 or more, go to **194**.

82 Make an Agility FEAT roll. If the result is 12 or less, go to **67**. If it's 13 or more, go to **92**.

83 Your actions are as quick as your realization, as you leap with all your radioactive spider-speed. The rest of the ceiling in the office collapses behind you, fire licking at your heels.

Landing in the next office, you discover the frantic woman hiding under a desk.

Go to **93**.

84 You try to leap out of the way but you're just a hair too slow. The blast from the pumpkin bomb hurls you against the wall and you sustain 10 points of damage.

If this reduces your Health score to 0, it's good-bye Spidey. Otherwise, go to **5**.

85 You hesitate, trying to pin down just what's happening—when there's danger all around, you don't know what to do first. And at that moment it's like the world has just collapsed on top of you.

Actually, the ceiling is caving in, flames licking down. Caught flat-footed, you start to get out of the way but you're a hair too slow. You go down under the collapsing ceiling. Your eyes sting under your mask and, angry at yourself, you shove the debris off you (but not before sustaining 8 points of health damage).

You stagger to your feet and plunge through the door into the next office. There, you discover the frantic woman hiding under a desk.

Go to **93**.

"I'm outa here," you say, leaping away. In- **86** furiated, the Hobgoblin raises a fist and reaches for a pumpkin bomb—just as the oncoming train crashes into him, reducing him to the mystic dust from which he came.

Go to **18**.

When you took wedding vows, you swore **87** it was for better or worse—and it's not going to get much worse than this.

You scoop Mary Jane up in your arms and face the Rhino.

"Using her as a shield?" shouts the Rhino. "I'll crush the both of you."

"Fat chance, fatso," you shout.

The Rhino charges at you but you're already moving. You bound across the arena as if you were on the moon, so little effect does the gravity seem to have on you.

You run through the open gate through which the Rhino had entered. "Hang on, MJ," you say. "I'm getting you out of here."

There's no response, and you fight down a surge of panic.

You run through a narrow corridor and a centurion steps into your way, but you don't even slow down, running right over him, flattening him.

Go to **97**.

88 Lying flat on the rooftop, you don't even breathe as one of those less-than-friendly ghosts passes over you without spotting you. But you can't count on your luck holding out forever.

Several things occur to you, almost at the same time. First, this situation is way, way out of your league. It needs some genuine world-beaters called in, like the Avengers. They're the world's mightiest super-heroes, after all, and you know where Avengers' Mansion is. You could get over there and get their help, no sweat. Give them the amulet and get the heck out of this situation.

Second, the ghosts, or demons as that creep had called them, are all looking for Spider-Man. But they don't know Peter Parker from a hole in the wall. If you can get home and change to Peter Parker, it will at least give you some time to get your head together—try to sort this craziness out.

Third, you can still hear the amulet whispering in your mind. Calling you, telling you of the power that's still at hand and available to you. You wonder if you could possibly use this amulet to find Doctor Strange, wherever he might be hidden. It's a possibility, you suppose.

If you want to head to Avengers' Mansion and get some big-league help, go to **131**. If you want to make your way home, change to Peter Parker and get some time to sort this out, go to **9**. If you want to try to use the amulet to locate Doc, go to **49**.

I don't know what this thing is capable of, **89** you think frantically, *and I don't want to find out.*

Quickly turning and firing a webline, you start to swing away. Your spider-sense tells you that the ghost is starting after you—and at that moment, a bolt of mystic energy flies past your shoulder. You turn in shock and look behind you to see the ghost dying, if that's possible. Its translucent, ethereal body crisps and turns in on itself. Within seconds, it has been reduced to a randomly dispersed bit of smoke.

Go to **99**.

Something is definitely wrong. The frus- **90** trating thing is, it's nothing you can put your finger on. Nevertheless, something tells you that things aren't as they appear, and whatever Doc is about to tell you, you're going to be extremely careful in proceeding on that basis. Add 3 Karma points for your intuitive caution, and go to **100**.

91   The world turns topsy-turvy around you.
Stop the universe. I want to get off, you think.
You've gone dimension hopping before, usually
with some crazy caper that Doctor Strange involved you in. Maybe you shouldn't complain
about the disorientation. After all, Doc does this
kind of stuff all the time.

By the same token, you manage to think, as you
are surrounded by a dazzling array of colors, *the
chances are real good that Stephen Strange
wouldn't be able to swing around the world by his
pinkies on tiny little strands of webbing.*

Suddenly, the world stops swirling, though not
within your head, and you land with a bone-
jarring thud.

Go to **2**.

You bound out of the Rhino's way as he **92** charge's past, and the breeze of his passing almost knocks you flat.

Unable to halt his full-steam charge, the Rhino smashes into the wall behind you. His horn is momentarily stuck.

For the next couple of seconds, the Rhino is occupied with dislodging himself. You could pound on him, but that would probably have no effect—his gray hide could withstand you for the brief time you'd have.

However, there are two other possibilities. Mary Jane is still tied to that stake, and now would be a good time to free her. Also, the emperor is sitting up in his box, shouting for the Rhino to break free and turn you into spectacular spider-burger. You can't shake the feeling that somehow the emperor is the key to all this.

Do you want to run to Mary Jane and try to set her loose (**130**), or take the opportunity to head toward the emperor (**3**)?

"There you are!" you say, letting out a **93** breath, then realizing that that wasn't the brightest move. Still, she looks so panic-stricken that she probably wouldn't have come with you anyway if you had taken some sort of friendly approach.

You look around and realize that you have a definite problem—this office is a corner office, and there's no window. "I sure wouldn't put up with an office with no window," you say. Looking back, you see the office you just came from now impassable from the collapsed ceiling. Your only way out is through the door of this office.

You pick up the woman, shouting, "Hold on!"

"Wait!" she shrieks. "I've read about you! Don't—"

"If you don't shut up, you won't be reading about anyone in the future," you snap. Slinging her over your shoulder, you rip open the door. There's a huge exhibit area spread out in front of you. One case is cracked open, and the rest are about to be consumed. Can't worry about that now. Over on the opposite corner you spot a fire door.

You leap over the flames, smoke choking you and tearing your eyes. When you get to the door, you discover that several huge lengths of chain are wrapped around in front of it, blocking the exit.

"Who's the genius who blocked the fire exit?!" you shout.

"Security problems!" replies the woman whose life you're trying to save.

You have no time for subtleties, and slam into the door.

Make a Strength FEAT roll. If the result is 11 or less, go to **6**. If it is 12, go to **106**. If it is 13 or more, go to **4**.

94   The ersatz Doctor Strange staggers under the mystic assault of the young woman, but already begins to mount a defense, when you leap forward and slam your fist into him. The punch hurls him to one side.

Unfortunately, he falls next to the dropped amulet. With a cry of triumph, he grabs it and clutches it to his body.

76

"Fools!" he shouts, pulling himself up. "You think you've won? You've only got a temporary stay of execution." Then he vanishes, with the amulet, and with the frozen form of Doctor Strange.

Go to **215**.

You try to leap clear of the falling debris **95** and you almost make it. But a collapsing beam catches you in the leg, pain searing through your thigh. Still, it could have been a lot worse. (You sustain 2 points of health damage.)

You lurch to your feet, walking slowly, with a limp. But your recuperative powers are quick— it'll only take you a few moments to fully recover your speed.

Treating your leg gingerly, you move into the next office as the rest of the ceiling comes down behind you. In the office, you find the frantic woman hiding under a desk.

Go to **93**.

You try leaping out of his way, but the Hulk **96** is much faster now than he used to be. He snags one of your legs in his grasp, tightens his grip, and snaps you around.

"Time to crack the whip!" he says and hurls you the length of the Coliseum.

Traveling with a speed just short of a guided missile, you crack into the far wall and slide to the ground. The world spins around you like a gigantic top.

Subtract 10 points from your Health score. If that brings your total down to 0, say goodnight, Spidey. Otherwise, go to **7**.

97   You run outside the Coliseum, Mary Jane cradled limply in your arms. And—are you imagining it, or is she actually starting to feel lighter? More insubstantial? Almost as if—

And MJ vanishes.

You stand there, staring at your empty arms. The shouting of the capacity crowd behind you in the Coliseum also disappears.

Everything is quiet and calm.

"Well that's beautiful. Just beautiful," you say to yourself angrily.

Obviously, the entire thing had been an hallucination—one that you were dragged into when you came in physical contact with that guy who turned into the emperor. It must be as if he were one half of a circuit, and when you touched him it was completed and all hell broke loose.

Well, they're not going to get you the same way again. Fists clenched, you turn and stalk back into the Coliseum.

The moment you enter, you hear that same voice shouting "Help me! Someone please help me."

You turn away and head toward **52**.

You make absolutely no move against **98**
Mordo. Instead, you leap directly toward Doctor
Strange, so quickly that he doesn't have time to
prepare. A right to the jaw and immediately the
master magician loses consciousness.

Mordo stands there, the amulet in his hand, and
he laughs loudly and triumphantly, "I've done it!
I've won! At last, I've won." Then he turns and,
looking at you, smiles. "And you—you have as-
sisted me well. From now on, you shall be my
good and faithful servant."

He looks down, notices that Clea still has some
fight in her, and effortlessly knocks her out with
one chop of his hand.

What a wonderful master he is, you think. How
wonderful that someone finally appreciates you
as Spider-Man and gives you the kind of attention
and respect you deserve. And you are happy.

You turn to see a woman hovering noncha- **99**
lantly nearby. She is stunning, with hair of silver,
and clad in a purple and red body stocking.

"Hello, Spider-Man," she says. "Stephen
Strange sent me."

"How do I know?" you ask warily.

She shrugs. "Don't believe me. I can follow you
around unseen if I wish. You won't remain as
Spider-Man forever—eventually you'll have to return home. But that will take too much time, and
I'd like your help as well. So—can we talk?"

"Great," you mutter. "First I get dragged into
some crazy mystic mess, and now I have to trust a
floating comedienne. All right, Silver—let's talk."

Go to **110**.

100   "How's it going, Doc? Pull any rabbits out of a hat lately? And where's Wong?"

Sounding slightly distant, Doctor Strange says, "My manservant had a pressing engagement elsewhere. However, Spider-Man, as you suspect, we have rather pressing matters ourselves to discuss."

He steps back and you enter his home. Strange stands to one side and the door closes, as if pulled on invisible string. With all your previous encounters with Doc, that seems to be one of the more mild exhibitions of his mystical prowess.

Turning to him, you can't help but notice that he looks more strained, more "out of it" than usual. "You want to tell me what's going on, Doc?"

Doctor Strange crosses his legs under himself, going into a lotus position. "You want to discuss this up in your Sanctum, Doc?" you ask, referring to his mystical "office" in the upper reaches of the townhouse. It's where he keeps his assorted tomes, and the weird globe that lets him look all over Earth—it's his power base.

"No," he says quickly. "There isn't time. What we have to discuss cannot be delayed as much as a moment."

"Whoa, lighten up, Doc. What's going on?"

He frowns in concentration for a moment, and then says, "There was a fire earlier. You are aware of it?"

"So you *are* involved with that!"

"Yes. As you may or may not know, that building was the Ditko Museum of Mystic Artifacts. Many of the objects they've acquired there are trinkets. 'Magic' rocks, charms, that sort of thing. Recently, however, an archaeologist uncovered

80

something that is hardly a trinket."

You wait for him to continue, but he closes his eyes and grunts softly. "Hey, Doc, you need some Pepto or something?"

"Quiet!" he says, very brusquely. "I'm concentrating." Then, moments later, he appears to compose himself, and says, "The object is called the Caputo amulet. A disk of about this size," and he approximates the size with his hands. "It has mystic markings on it, written in a tongue that hasn't been spoken for more than 2,500 years. The mystic energy it controls is enough to lay waste to the entire planet. It could reduce Earth to a cinder."

You let out a low whistle. "If this thing is so powerful, why wasn't it simply destroyed?"

"It can't be destroyed," Strange replies. "Twelve of the most powerful sorcerers on Earth combined, centuries ago, to divide it into four sections. They did so at the cost of the lives of eight of them, so fiercely did the amulet fight back. The four remaining sorcerers took the four pieces and scattered them around the planet. Each piece was powerful in and of itself, but could be contained. The pieces are now in Rome, London, Morocco, and . . . the fourth—was lost."

"Lost?!"

"The city was buried under the flow of an erupting volcano," said Strange. "Still, that hardly seemed to matter, because the idea was to make certain that they remained undiscovered and unjoined.

"One piece, as I said, was found, however, in an archaelogical dig. It was brought to the Ditko Museum for study—and it was there that my greatest enemy, Baron Mordo, detected its presence at about the same time I did. We battled for possession of the quarter of the amulet. The result was the conflagration of this morning."

"And the piece of the amulet?"

Strange takes a long sigh. "Mordo—has it."

"What?"

"I'm afraid so," says Strange. "That is why you are needed. You must retrieve the other three quarters of the amulet."

"Whoa, hey, wait a minute," you say. "You don't need me. You need Indiana Jones."

As if you hadn't spoken, Strange says, "The remaining three pieces—in London, Rome and Morocco—are protected by mystic wards. They are keyed to their attacker's own mind. Whatever your own greatest fears or opponents are, these are what will oppose you. They are only creations of the mystic barriers so do not be concerned about injuring them."

"What about them injuring me?!" you say in alarm. "This is ridiculous. Can't you handle this, Doc?"

"I cannot leave," replies Doc. "That is why I have been so distracted. Mordo, with the aid of the single quarter of the amulet, has imprisoned me within my own domicile. I have been trying to break through the mystic wards, but have been unsuccessful. Only my spirit form can penetrate it, and that is useless in this instance. You, however, can come and go as you like, for the wards are created only to imprison a mystic like myself. Please, Spider-Man, the only hope I have of overcoming Mordo is by obtaining those other three pieces. Combined, they will give me more than enough power. But you must hurry. At the moment, Mordo must not know where the other three pieces are, but he may be able to use the one piece he has to trace them. With one piece, Mordo could put a city into flames. With all four, . . ."

"All right," you say, putting up your hands. "I'm in, already. But how am I supposed to get to these places? Hop in my private jet?"

"I can transport you mystically," says Strange. "And once there, my spirit form will be able to point the way. Beyond that, I cannot do."

"Okay, okay. Can't have the world go up in flames. It'll ruin property values. Where do I go first?"

"That is up to you, my friend."

If you want to go to London first, go to **111**. If you want to meander to Rome, then go to **91**. If you're on the road to Morocco, go to **119**.

Bursting with confidence, you walk over **101** to Clea. Looking back on your life, you think about all the times you were uncertain. *How,* you wonder, *could I ever have had any uncertainties? Any doubts that anything I did was absolutely, indisputably right?*

You look over at Doc, in his comatose state, ready to free him with the amulet. Then, to your surprise, he again vanishes.

"Cat and mouse, huh, Mordo?" you murmur to yourself. "Fine. Enjoy your little tricks, your little maneuvers. You won't be able to enjoy them much longer."

You've never felt so confident. Always, in battle, you've used your wisecracks and jokes to cover the uncertainties you've felt. To try to avoid dealing with the fact that you're fighting people who are trying to kill you. Not anymore, however. Now you know that, when you face Mordo, you can wipe up the floor with him.

You take Clea by the shoulder and slowly she opens her eyes. "Stephen?" She sits up slowly, fighting the chill going through her.

"He's gone," you say. "Vanished again. It must be another maneuver from Mordo—the last one he's going to make."

You hold the amulet to her. "Get us to Doc. I'll take it from there."

She stares at the amulet, almost in fear. "I—I can't—"

"You have to!" you say urgently. "I don't know how to make this thing work. You do. If you don t get us out of here, we're going to wind up as icicles. You've got to get us moving, quickly—while you've still got the strength to do it."

She nods, knowing the truth of what you're saying. Taking a deep breath, she grasps the amulet while you hold it and concentrates. Her eyes narrow to slits, and her face becomes even more drawn than it was before.

"I've—I've found him," she manages to say. "Let's—let's go get him."

The world again upends around you, and for the first time, it doesn't bother you in the least.

Go to **11**.

102   With a sigh, you say, "Look, MJ—I don't think I should pass this up. If there's anything I can do to help out there, I really can't just turn my back."

And then you add brightly, "Besides—maybe whatever's going on will make some good news photos for the *Daily Bugle*."

MJ sighs, but smiles. "Well," she says, "as long as you're doing it for good, solid capitalist reasons, and not just out of the goodness of your heart."

"Heaven forbid," you say and give her a quick kiss before heading into the bathroom. Give yourself 2 Karma points for your resolve.

Moments later, you're in your Spidey outfit and climbing out the skylight exit in your bathroom. You hear from within the apartment, just as you leave, the voices of the three women who live next door. You can't make out what they're saying, but it doesn't matter. You're on your way.

Up on the roof, you fire a webline and swing out across the street. One more police car barrels past beneath you. *Whatever's going down, it must be pretty big,* you think to yourself. Big enough that, with the right pictures, old Jonah will actually unlock the big vault at the *Bugle* and pay you, for once, what your photos are really worth.

Effortlessly, you keep pace with the police car and then the morning breeze wafts toward you the reason for their haste—a fire. And sure enough, you pass a fire engine that's stuck in absolutely unmoving Manhattan traffic. The drivers are frantically trying to get out of the way, but the streets are wall-to-wall cars.

Go to **30**.

"Okay, Silver," you say, flipping her the **103** amulet as if it were a poker chip. "We'll play it your way for now."

Alarmed at your nonchalant toss of the amulet, she grabs at it in an entertainingly desperate leap.

"You idiot!" she says, cradling the amulet. "How can you toss this around?"

"Mordo told me that it took a dozen sorcerors to split the thing apart," you say. "Even if I'd really allowed it to fall—which I wouldn't have 'cause I could have snared it with a webline—could that fall have damaged it?"

She glares at you for a moment, then abruptly her face softens slightly. "Probably not," she admits. And for the first time, she smiles.

You begin to appreciate the strain she's been under, the concern she obviously has for Strange, and you resolve to try to lay off the snappy patter for a while. Add 1 Karma point to your total for being concerned about her feelings.

"Now," says Clea, snapping her legs into a lotus position, "it's not something I could do on my own, but with my power augmented by this amulet, I believe that I can find Stephen."

She stares intently into the amulet, so intently that you're tempted to ask her if there will be a quiz on it next period. Then you remind yourself of your promise to cool the wisecracks.

She studies the amulet, and although she's making no move at all, it's clear that she's exerting effort. Her breathing becomes strained and irregular, her forehead is beaded in sweat. And the amulet begins to glow.

You start to become alarmed and, even though she'll probably bawl you out for it, you go over and shake her roughly. "Clea! Clea, snap out of it!" She turns, blinking at you, no recognition in her eyes at first. Then, slowly, she returns to normal.

"Are you okay?" you ask urgently. "It looked like—like that thing was sucking something out of you."

"That—is possible," she says. "Apparently, those who try to use the power of the amulet—those mystically trained—face a danger of having some of their own ability and individuality leached from them."

"You mean we could have just let old Mordo use the thing and he probably would have fried his own brains?"

"Possibly," she says. "The amulet's influence is a subtle thing. If you're on guard against it, and your mind is mystically trained, you can resist it. Come," and she grasps your hand, "we're going after Stephen. Right now."

"Are you sure you're up to—" Suddenly the world lurches away and spins beneath you.

Go to **40**.

104   *If I hang around here, they'll probably figure out some way to blame me for the fire,* you think sourly, as you swing up to the rooftop nearby. Your camera is where you left it. You take a few quick shots, although now that the firefighters have extinguished much of the blaze it's not nearly as exciting as it was.

You swing off to the *Daily Bugle,* stopping very quickly at home to grab a change of clothes which you web onto your back.

Once at the *Bugle* you change to Peter Parker and trot down the stairwell to the city room. There, you're confronted by Kathryn Cushing, the *Bugle's* city editor. You sigh inwardly. Things were much easier when you were selling your pics to Jonah Jameson. Masochistically, Spidey's biggest detractor was always willing to buy photos of your web-slinging alter ego, probably so he could go over them with a microscope and try to find Spidey involved in some sort of wrongdoing.

Kate Cushing, however, couldn't care less about Spider-Man, and it's really been tough to sell her your pictures because you still don't have the technical finesse that she wants to see.

You hold up the roll of film. "Pictures of the fire downtown, Kate," you say enthusiastically.

She peers over the top of her glasses. "Anyone killed?"

"Uh—no. But Spider-Man—"

"Was *he* killed?"

"No."

"That's not news. You want to photograph fires, go work for TV. They love that stuff."

You're about to make a sharp retort when a scream snaps your head around. To your shock, the ghostly form of Doctor Strange is wafting through the city room!

Reporters and secretaries scatter right and left as the ectoplasmic body of the master magician sails through, looking around as if seeking someone. It silently glides through a wall and out of the building.

Go to **142**.

Reflexively, desperately, not even sure **105** why you're doing it, you hold the amulet up in front of you.

"Back off, Doc!" you shout, "Or I'll toss this mystic frisbee at you."

He screams in fury.

You're stunned. You've worked with Doc a number of times before, and in every instance he was a perfect picture of calm, of confidence. Now he's acting like a lunatic. Could it be that—

Bolts of mystic energy fly toward you as you hold the amulet in front of you, feeling like a two-bit Captain America.

And to your shock, the amulet glows red-hot.

Under your mask, your lips curl back in pain as the power of the amulet shoots all the way up your arm. It attracts the lambent power that Strange is hurling at you, attracts it like a magnet—and absorbs it.

Again and again Doc tries one spell after another on you, and the amulet absorbs them all. Slowly, you back up. Somehow, miraculously, you're impervious to this mystic assault. But you don't know how long it's going to last, and you sure don't want to hang around to find out. You leap toward the steps, keeping the amulet between you and the infuriated mage.

"Come back here!" shouts Strange. "Come back here so that I can kill you!"

"Sorry if I have to pass on your charming invitation, Doc," you reply, "but my social calendar's booked up through next Thursday. I can't possibly die before then."

You turn and bolt up the stairs.

Go to **108**.

106

The door flies open from the impact, with the chain cracking sounding like a cannon shot. But you've used the last of your strength to do it. Clearly, the fire took more out of you than you thought. You slump forward, half-hanging out the door, which opens onto a fire escape stairway. Then the woman you intended to save steps over your fallen body. "You wanna—give me a hand?" you call, but without a backward glance she runs down the stairs, leaving you to the mercy of the flames.

Nice kid, you think. *Wouldn't want my cousin to marry her, though.* You start to pull yourself to your feet and as you do so, firefighters are charg-

ing up the stairs.

Gratefully, you accept their help. All the way down the stairs you feel like a world-class fool for getting into this situation. Go with the feeling, and deduct 1 Karma point.

Your rescuers bring you around to the front of the building and you find someone waiting there for you.

Go to **50**.

107 You put everything you've got into it as you smash your fist into the Hulk's face.

He doesn't even move. "Nice punch," he says, rubbing his jaw. "Now try one of mine."

Go to **213**.

108 The stairway seems to tilt at a bizarre angle, but for someone who can stick to walls, that's hardly a handicap.

Your mind races furiously as you barrel up the stairs, taking five at a time. You're starting to come up with answers that you're quite sure you don't like.

As near as you can tell, there are two possibilities. Either Doc Strange has completely lost his mind, or that's not Doc Strange.

But then why didn't your spider-sense start going nuts the moment you got near him? Possibly, your opponent has some sort of mystic ability that dampened your spider-sense.

Well, why not? It's pretty obvious at this point that whoever you're facing is definitely a high-caliber magician.

And at that moment, bands of mystic energy

appear in front of you.

They're almost hypnotically beautiful, scarlet bands that block your path. Do you try to use the amulet against them (**220**), or do you try to find some other way (**182**)?

Leaping out onto the roof, you quickly **109** jump over to the adjacent building to try to draw your pursuer after you.

And sure enough, here she comes, effortlessly floating after you. . . . *She?*

Yes, most definitely a "she." Her hair is silver, kind of like the Black Cat's. Her outfit is skintight, her shirt is purple and netted, her pants crimson and covered with an intricate lined pattern.

Do you try to use your webbing on her (**224**), or try to run from her (**59**)?

"Now listen carefully," she says. "We **110** don't have a lot of time. My name is Clea. Once I was Doctor Strange's—disciple. Now, however, I am the ruler of the Dark Dimension."

"Oh, *that* Clea," you reply. "The Dark Dimension. Of course. That's two doors down from the Goodness and Light Dimension, isn't it?"

She sighs and shakes her head, muttering something about mortals being fools. "Since Stephen summoned me to his aid, I have managed to determine this much. He was attacked and, because of Mordo's possession of one-quarter of the Caputo amulet, he was defeated by Mordo."

"So Mordo was the one I was dealing with the whole time," you say. "That explains why my spider-sense kept bugging me."

"It would have been a far more strident warning if Mordo hadn't dampened it," she tells you. "The amulet that he sent you after is a sort of—to put it in a way you'd understand—a mystic battery. It absorbs mystic energy, stores it, then releases it— usually in the form of flame. With a small amount of energy, the Caputo amulet could lay waste to a city. Fully charged, it could reduce Earth to a cinder."

"Why would this Mordo guy want to burn up the whole planet?" you ask. "It's his world, too."

"With the Caputo amulet in his hands he could travel to any one of an infinite number of dimensions. He would have no need of Earth."

"Well, I think I need Earth for a little while longer," you say. "So what do we do now?"

"That," replies Clea, "is obvious. Our only hope is to find and free Doctor Strange. Mordo has sent him somewhere, and as soon as we locate him, he can use the amulet sections you've acquired to their full potential and overcome Mordo."

"It works for me," you reply.

Go to **200**.

111   There is a wild disorientation around you and the feeling that you should have stayed in bed this morning. *Considering what was waiting for me*, you think, *I must have been crazy not to.* It's the only thought that you can muster, as you find yourself in a maze of colors that threatens to put your brain on overload.

Then, abruptly, the world stops spinning, and you find yourself right in front of a honking car.

You're startled, about to leap out of the way, when you realize that the car isn't moving. For that matter, there's a car directly behind you that isn't moving either. You're smack in the middle of a London traffic jam.

You know it's London, because a man sticks his head out the car window and calls in a crisp British accent, "Oh dear fellow? Would you mind possibly moving, in the off-chance that the automobile traffic in this lane should happen to begin flowing again?"

How can I resist an offer like that? you think, and bound out of the way.

You look around, uncertain of which way to go—but then you spot him, as big as life—well, not exactly life.

Doctor Strange's ectoplasmic spirit is floating near the entrance to the underground—London's equivalent of the subway.

All right, you think. *The subway it is, then.*

You're about to head toward it, when two things happen: Strange's ectoplasmic form disappears, his face wincing in pain, and a crisp voice speaks from behind you.

"I say! What's all this?"

You turn, and a brusque-looking London police officer, a bobby, stands there, rocking back and forth slowly on his heels, gently tapping his truncheon in the palm of one hand.

"Would you like to tell me," he asks in a no-nonsense voice, "just who the devil you think you're made out to be?"

If you want to ask the bobby who *he* thinks you're made out to be, go to **12**. If you don't want to waste time, and immediately prove who you are, and that what you're doing is important, go to **54**.

112   Slowly, you open your eyes, half-praying that you're going to wake up in your nice, soft bed at home.

But then the cold cuts through you and you come to the horrible realization that everything you experienced was real. As you slowly stagger to your feet, you find that not only were things as bad as you thought they were, but actually worse.

Doc Strange is gone.

Clea is gone.

The creature is gone.

The amulet is gone.

The only one still around is you, and you're not in such hot shape right now.

The winds roar around you, and you realize you've been abandoned in the Himalayas.

But Mordo, and the monster for that matter, have made a serious mistake. They've left you alive. It's a mistake that others have made, only to learn that Spider-Man is not someone to count out as long as he's drawing breath. Even if it is chilly, snow-filled breath.

You start forward through the snow, knowing that you'll persevere—that you will eventually make it back, somehow. And when you do, Mordo better watch his back.

113   Before Clea catches the quarter-amulet, a gloved hand catches it in midair.

"I wouldn't," says a calm, confident voice.

Clea turns, her eyes widening in pleased surprise. "Stephen! You broke free on your own."

"It was only a matter of time," Strange replies. "One of Mordo's abilities could not hold me indefinitely."

Smiling, Clea says, "I feel as if I could."

She embraces him and, for the only time you can remember, Doc acts just like a regular guy, as he returns the embrace. He looks over Clea's shoulder at you and his moustache twitches into a very small smile.

"Hey, looks like you got things under control here," you say. "I'm outa here."

"Spider-Man," Clea says. "I—misjudged you. I'm very sorry."

"That's okay. Everybody does. It goes with the territory. Just go put in a good word for me with J. Jonah Jameson."

"I—do not know him," Clea says slowly. "But if you think it would help."

"Nope," you say. "Not in the least little bit." With that, you let yourself out the front door.

As you think over what you've been through, it occurs to you that the amulet was exerting some sort of unhealthy influence on you. But you don't have to be concerned with it anymore—now it's Doc's problem, and the physician will be cordially invited to heal himself.

Rubbing your slightly bruised knuckles, you fire a webline and swing off into the night.

The air around you seems to crackle, **114** burning from the energies that are being unleashed. But you now realize something. With all the power that Doc's tossing around, he has yet to make a direct shot at you. Why won't he, or . . .

Slowly, you look down at the amulet in your hand. Is it possible that he just can't? That somehow this amulet protects you from direct mystical attack?

Of course! That has to be it. Give yourself 2 Karma points for the realization, and go to **124**.

115   It's a good leap, but your timing is off, and it carries you past the fallen amulet.

"Ha!" cries the fake Doc Strange, grabbing up the amulet and waving his hand, freezing you in place. "I could kill you right now!" he shouts, "But why rush? With the Caputo amulet in my grasp, the entire world will be mine, and you'll never be able to run far enough."

With those triumphant words, he vanishes, taking the paralyzed form of the real Doc Strange with him.

Go to **215**.

116   All the uncertainties slip away from you like droplets off a leaf.

Yes. Yes, it's all perfect. Everything makes so much sense now. This is what your entire life has been in preparation for. This is what you've wanted, what you've deserved. This is what all the hardship you've endured is for—this ultimate culmination. The ultimate power, and the ultimate responsibility.

Furious, Mordo leaps at you and you look at him. He seems so pitiful now. You make the smallest gesture and suddenly Mordo is gone. Banished. You couldn't care less about where.

You turn and Doctor Strange is behind you, shouting something to you. It doesn't matter. He doesn't matter.

You walk toward the ceiling and Strange hurls mystic bolts at you. It annoys you, but you seem to recall that he was a friend of yours once. So you absorb the attack, rather than turning it back on him and obliterating him where he stands. He shouts, "Spider-Man!" but you're no longer Spider-Man. You are above him. Spider-Man was but the child—you are the adult.

You walk up and out of the house, passing through walls as if they were not there. You walk up into the evening sky, no longer needing that shoddy webbing to make your way around. Now the air is your home, your supporter.

Finally, you are at peace. No more problems, no more hang-ups. No more difficulties. Except—

One thing bothers you. It is dark. And you must have light—there must always be light.

You absorb all the magic energies from throughout the world, wherever they may be. You feel the power swelling within you. There is nothing that you cannot do. Nothing.

You reach out, gathering the planet to you, and start moving it closer to the sun. Turning the side of the planet, you face the greatness of that ball of fire.

Let there be light, you think.

You feel the heat and light wash over you, and you smile.

And it is good.

Moments later, you arrive at Doc's home **117** and this time you go back in through the skylight that you'd exited from. You crawl slowly along the walls, your spider-sense alert to danger. As you cling to the walls, you become aware that the place seems to be tilting, almost as if the walls are angling toward each other. The other weird aspect about this joint is that the insides always appear to take up much more room than the outsides could possibly accommodate.

You make your way to what you believe is a downstairs study (although things are so unusual in this place that for all you know you might be upstairs again). There are hardwood floors and tall bookshelves.

You pull a book down at random, wondering what bizarre and arcane lore it is filled with, but find that you're staring at a copy of *Gray's Anatomy*. You shrug. Well, he is supposed to be a doctor. You slide the book back into place on the shelf—and your spider-sense abruptly warns you of danger behind you.

You whirl to see Mordo standing there, completely nonchalant.

"Looking for me?" he asks.

Go to **127**.

118 "I've done it!" he shrieks. "I have the Caputo amulet. Now nothing on Earth can stop me!"

"Hold the phone," you say angrily. "Haven't you forgotten about your little old webslinger?"

"Not at all," he says, and suddenly eldritch energy fills the room.

You have just been transformed into a bottle of liquid drain cleaner. Your entire adventure has gone down the drain.

119 The world twists and turns around you. You feel as if you're some small particle or speck that's trapped in a whirlpool of water swirling

down a drain.

"What a way to run an airline," you say, and you notice in a distant sort of way that your words vanish as if you never spoke.

And suddenly, you stop falling, landing with a thud.

When you were a kid, one of your favorite activities was to spin around as fast as you could and then suddenly stop. The world would continue to whirl about you and you would always fall over laughing. That sensation is pretty much how you feel now, except you don't feel like laughing.

Gimme a break, you think to yourself as the world around you slowly rights itself. The Middle Eastern sun beats down on you as you stagger to your feet.

Looking around, you expect to see the Morocco

you've always seen in movies. Small, cramped, crowded with Arabs in long flowing clothes.

Instead, you are looking at a fairly modern city. You blink in surprise—this was not what you had anticipated at all. Several tourists point and snap your picture. "Love your costume!" They call to you, and you realize from their accents that they're American. "Someplace around here selling those Spider-Man outfits?"

"Uh, yeah. Abdul's House of Heroes," you say.

"Really? Where's that?"

"Right where it's always been," you reply quickly, moving off before they can ask any more uncomfortable questions.

Two kids immediately come up to you, and the larger one says, "Please, mister. We are poor, my mother needs an operation and my brother is pregnant—"

"Sister!" hisses the smaller one.

"Nice line, guys," you say, "but I don't have pockets in this outfit anyway. Sorry."

You turn, fire a webline at a nearby building, and swing off, leaving the kids in open-mouthed astonishment.

You web across the city, waiting for some sign of what you should do next. You start humming "The Road to Morocco," then, abruptly, you find yourself swinging straight through Doc Strange's hovering ectoplasmic form.

Go to **129**.

120 Interlude—
There is, someplace beyond the understanding of a mere mortal, another dimension, as close to ours as a passing dream, as far away as the far-

thest star. And in that dimension, a young woman sits quietly, thoughtfully, thinking of another world in which she once dwelled. A man who was once hers to have and hold and love, but whom she ultimately had to let go in order to fulfill herself. To meet her responsibilities—responsibilities which eventually led to her leading this strange and besieged realm.

What is he doing these days? she wonders silently. *Is he safe? Is he well? Is he even alive—yes. He must be, for if something happened to him somehow, in some manner, I would know it.*

Then, to her shock, a figure begins to coalesce in front of her. She blinks, uncertain of what she is about to see . . . and then she recognizes him.

"Stephen?" she whispers.

His image is hazy and faint, as if he's fighting to make his form visible. Something, some powerful spell, is interfering with his expression. His mouth doesn't even move—it doesn't need to in order to communicate with her.

"Trapped," he manages to say. "Find—Spider-Man. He has—has—"

And then he vanishes.

—End of Interlude.

Go to **199**.

You make it to the top of the stairs, your **121** chest heaving, certain that pursuit will continue at any moment. You glance around quickly and there, in the ceiling overhead, is a clearly glowing symbol of the amulet—a circle divided into quarters.

You leap up, adhering easily to the ceiling and put your fist through the symbol. Reaching

around inside, you grasp something hard and triangular.

"Come to papa, baby," you mutter, and pull the
quarter-amulet out of its hiding place. You stare at
the piece of stone. It seems to pulsate softly in
your hand—but how could something that's little
more than rock be pulsating?

At that moment, Doc Strange materializes in
front of you, nodding approvingly. Behind you, all
sound has ceased—obviously, as soon as you got
your hands on the piece of amulet, the mystic defenses assumed that you were able to handle it
and halted their attack.

Go to **241**.

122 "It might be some sort of trick," you say
to yourself. "Then again, it might not. Either way,
I can't afford to take the chance."

Go to **32**.

123 Mustering all your strength, all your determination, you leap forward, hands outstretched toward Mordo.

But you aren't able to get enough forward motion on the jump, and because you're no longer
anchored, the winds pick you up and hurl you like
a poker chip, toward a far wall. You swiftly land
with your feet planted against it. Then, like an ex-
pert swimmer, you hurl yourself forward through
the winds, and land next to the imprisoned Doc
Strange.

The winds are already losing their power—an
indication of Mordo's rapidly dwindling force. But
there's no sense in taking any chances with him—

especially when the means to free Doc is right here at hand.

You swing the amulet around, ready to slam it into the mystic field that holds Doc prisoner. From across the room, Mordo shouts, "No! You don't know what you're doing! Absorbing the power from that field could be the mystic charge that fills the amulet to overflowing!"

"Oh, right. You lie to me every step of the way and now I'm supposed to believe you? Fat chance, Mordo."

Go to **152**.

You hold the amulet out in front of you **124** and you think of every spell you ever heard Doc spout, calling, "By the flames of Saltines, by the brains of Satannish, by Z.Z. Top's beard, let Doctor Strange vanish!"

For a moment, Doc halts his attack and stares at you in disbelief. "What?"

He's not half as confused as you are, but this is definitely the time to get while the getting is good. You turn quickly and bolt up the stairs, which appear to be the only way out of this joint.

You hear an angry yell behind you—hardly surprising, you guess.

And at that moment, bands of mystic energy appear in front of you. You hesitate only a moment, because you're prepared for them. You slam the mystic amulet forward and with a giant "fwooosh," the eye-searing magical barrier is gone.

"Hot socks!" you say as you continue up the stairs.

Go to **38**.

125   Your web shot is right on the mark, snagging the amulet. The fake Doc reacts with fury but you're too quick, yanking on the amulet and snapping it into your grasp.

"You looking for this, swifty?" you call tauntingly.

"You'll pay for that!" he shouts.

You start to reply, "Cash or credit?" but then with alarm you see that he's hurling one mean spell your way. You think you may just barely have time to kiss yourself goodbye.

Go to **135**.

126   You're distracted at the last instant by a sudden gesture from your mystical opponent and the web shot goes wide.

The Doc Strange impersonator doesn't give you a break either, as he begins to chant, concocting a spell with your name on it.

Make an Agility FEAT roll. If the result is 13 or less, go to **136**. If it's 14 or more, go to **146**.

127   He makes no effort to hide his true appearance now—and it's a shame because, to tell the truth, he's sure not going to win any beauty prizes.

He's more muscular, bulkier than Doctor Strange is. He sports a harsh-looking beard, and his jet-black hair is cut to a widow's peak on his high forehead.

His eyes, black as pitch, seem to flash as he says, "I have need of you to do my bidding."

You waver slightly. "Why? Are we going to an auction?" But you're barely able to get the re-

106

mark out as his eyes seem to fill the room.

Make a combined Intuition and Psyche FEAT roll, adding Karma if you wish. If the result is 21 or less, go to **138**. If the result is 22 or more, go to **137**.

"Look, you've made it abundantly clear **128** that you think I'm going to be useless for this," you say with some irritation.

"Not useless," says Clea. "It's just that you are obviously out of your depth here. You have no training in this sort of thing."

"Fine," you say, handing her the amulet. "Go off and rescue Doc, then. You're so hot you don't need me." You turn away, your arms folded and wait for her to say, "I'm sorry, Spider-Man. Of course I need you."

You stand that way for about ten, fifteen seconds before the silence prompts you to turn around. You discover that she's gone. Vanished without a trace.

"Son of a gun," you say. "She took me on my word."

Well, that's that. If she's as capable as she says she is, she'll be able to handle this whole mess herself. You're obviously out of it.

You fire a webline and go swinging off into the evening, not quite satisfied with such a bittersweet ending to your adventure.

Doc Strange silently gestures. You're **129** starting to feel a little like Scrooge, obeying the beckonings of the ghost of Christmas Yet To Come.

"Bah humbug," you say. "Lead on, Doc."

You swing across the city, following his speeding ethereal form. Below you, the complexion of Morocco begins to change, and you realize that even though much of the city is new and modern, there are older sections of the city as well.

Ahead of you is a section that is noted for its large wall, once a barrier against attackers from the desert. This, you remember now, is the legendary Casbah, as in, "Come with me to the Casbah."

At that moment, you hear below you a shout of "Stop, thief!" You glance down and see a small boy darting through the streets of the city, slippery as an eel, a pocketbook tucked securely under his arm.

Behind him, pursuing him futilely, is a very large woman, obviously a tourist, waving her arms madly and falling farther and farther behind.

You're about to go down to stop him, but Strange's spirit form gestures impatiently at your hesitation.

Do you decide to let the kid go (**232**), or ignore Strange's gesticulations and go after him (**139**)?

130   Effortlessly firing a webline, you swing across the length of the arena, easily beating the Rhino to his goal. Dropping next to MJ, you snap her bonds with one hand and she sags against you, moaning, "Peter—get me out of here."

The ground is shaking. The Rhino, having freed himself, is picking up speed. "MJ," you say desperately, "are you really here?"

"You know me, Tiger," she replies softly. "I'll go

anywhere—for a party. Especially a toga party."
Then her head slumps back. She's unconscious.

You can make MJ your first priority, and get the
heck out of there (**87**), or you can put her down
and meet the Rhino's attack (**203**).

"Definitely," you say. "This is definitely **131**
out of my league. And when I have something out
of my league, it's time to go to the big boys and
find out if they can come out and play."

You wait until you're certain that the ghostly
demons are nowhere around, then swing out
across Manhattan.

Below you, the city spreads itself out. You've always loved the feel of soaring above everything.

Everyone seems like bugs, skittering around pursuing their little, mundane lives. And you glide above it all, striding across them, your shadow encompassing them. You are so much stronger, so much more powerful than they are. You smile under your mask. If they only knew of the power that was yours to command.

The Avengers. They're supposed to be the most powerful beings on Earth. Captain America, Thor, the Wasp, Captain Marvel—all of them and more. On several occasions, you could tell them that it's time you were running the show. After all, you've been at it longer than any of them except for Cap and Thor. You're entitled. There should be seniority in these things.

You swing over the block where Avengers' Mansion stands, and you grind to a halt in mid-air. The mansion is gone.

Nothing remains but a huge pile of rubble. There are some workmen there, standing around staring at blueprints, and a foreman clearly pointing out where work should begin.

You swing down and drop next to the foreman. He glances at you and looks utterly blase. "Now which one are you?" he asks with not too much interest.

"Spider-Man," you reply in irritation. "Want to see my driver's license?"

"Nah, I believe you. Whatcha want?"

You stare at him in surprise. "The Avengers. What do you think?"

"I think you got a long wait, is what I think," the foreman says. "There was some sort of big blowout. Avengers took on some guys, Masters of Evil or something stupid like that. Whole shebang got trashed. We're supposed to be putting it back

111

together—all us good king's horses and king's men. But it's gonna be weeks before we've got everything up and running."

"Well," you gesture helplessly, "where are the Avengers?"

"How do I know? Do I look like their answering service?" He turns away, clearly feeling that the conversation is over, and you realize that it really is.

You don't even know where to begin looking for the Avengers. You might as well return to **88**, and try something else.

132   You make your web shot, and it's a good one. But Mordo moves just fast enough, yanking his fist away and pulling the quarter-amulet away from your shot.

"Powerless pultroon!" he shouts.

"Whoa!" you reply. "I'd be really steamed about that, if I knew what pultroon was."

Your spider-sense kicks in, as Mordo launches a mystic assault. You realize, though, that it's not much of an assault. He really has grown weaker. You backflip out of the path of the bolts of eldritch energy, landing some feet away, and realize that you are barely an arm's length from the unmoving form of Doc Strange.

The amulet glows warm in your hand and, instinctively, you realize that all you have to do is touch the amulet to the spell imprisoning Doc Strange to set him free.

You can see from the pained expression on Mordo's face that the same thing has occurred to him.

Go to **24**.

"Come on, Seymour!" you shout. "Let's **133** go! You and me, right here!"

The creature turns on you, his lips pulling back to reveal yellowed teeth under blackened gums. *This thing's a walking commercial for proper dental hygiene,* you think.

It lunges at you—but you're no longer there. Even with the wind cutting into you, slowing you down, you're still faster than the abominable snowman here. Leaping over his head, you land behind him, and grab up the amulet lying in the snow. You close your hand around it and immediately the warmth from it floods through you. The monster roars nearby, but that doesn't seem to matter anymore. Under your mask, you smile. Seymour is standing over you, reaching down, not believing that you've made this so easy. And as he reaches for you, he brushes against the amulet you're holding.

The creature immediately staggers back, shrieking in alarm. You watch in detached fascination as the amulet clearly drains away the creature's life.

It *was* a magically based creature—something Mordo must have set up in advance as a failsafe. But the amulet siphoned away the magical energy that gave it life, and did so with incredible speed.

Within seconds, the creature is a husk of fur—nothing else remaining. The amulet glows hot in your hand, suffusing your spirit.

You should be upset that this creature is dead. You've always valued life, no matter what kind. You should be saddened, however slightly, that this creature had to die. But you simply don't care. Instead, you take joy in the vanquishing of an opponent.

It's clear that somehow the amulet is exerting an unpleasant influence on you. Deduct 1 Karma point from your score, as a small part of your individuality is taken from you by the amulet.

Go to **101**.

134   Everything is blackness, darker than you thought possible.

The first thing that occurs to you is *Omigod, I'm blind.* Then you realize that that's hardly the case—you've got your eyes closed. You slowly open them, looking around carefully at your place of confinement.

It's not so bad, really. Fortunately for you, Doc isn't the type who keeps dungeons on the premises. It sure wouldn't be a way to make friends and influence people. But then again, neither is this. The room isn't so bad—ornately carved table and chairs, tapestry on the wall, no windows (it figures). If you were bound by ropes, you could break apart a chair and try to saw through the bonds. Or just snap the rope. Or a chain, if such a paltry thing as iron were keeping you prisoner.

But no, you discover as you try to scratch your nose. The bonds that are holding your hands firmly behind your back are mystical in nature. You don't realize it at first, because with the weight of the magic bonds and the feel of them, it seems as if your arms are trapped in solid metal sleeves, joined at the wrists.

But then you walk over to a mirror set into the wall and turn to get a better look at your hands. To your astonishment, nothing holds your hands at all. Nothing that you can see, anyway. But as this discovery prompts you to pull, with even greater

futility, at your bonds, you realize that not everything is tied up with what you can see.

Your legs are free, which means you can walk
up on the ceiling, but what good does that do?

No. What's going to count is if you can somehow break free of the invisible bonds.

Make a combined Strength and Psyche FEAT
roll, adding Karma beforehand if you wish. If the
result is 20 or less, go to **144**. If it is 21 or more, go
to **145**.

The spell, ebony and overpowering, **135**
strikes you, then vanishes. You yell as the amulet
heats up in your hand, sucking in all the eldritch
energy crackling around you. Incredibly, a small
voice in your head says, *Don't worry, I'll protect
you.*

The silver-haired woman advances on the infuriated Doc. "You should never have attacked
Stephen," she says angrily. Then, with a quick
gesture, both Stranges vanish.

Go to **185**.

You make a desperate, valiant leap, but **136**
it's just a shade slow. The spell overwhelms you.

You have been transformed into a 12-inch color
TV. The bad news is that your adventure is over.
The good news is that you get great reception.

Your mind screams a warning at you. **137**
*He's trying to hypnotize you! Do something, you
idiot!*

Quickly, you close your eyes and mentally fight

115

off the almost druglike effects of the hypnosis. You can still hear Mordo softly encouraging, "You'll do what I ask. I have need of you, in a great and noble cause," but his words have no real impact.

But because you're wearing a full face mask, Mordo doesn't know that. Keeping your eyes tightly shut, you slowly start walking forward. You make no sudden move, no abrupt gesture that would indicate to Mordo that you are not under his power. You avoid saying something stupid like "Yes, Master," because he would probably realize that you're still solidly in control of yourself.

Your ploy appears to be working, as you hear him murmur, "Yes, yes, that's right. You're going to be my weapon against Doctor Strange. You will catch him by surprise—"

As he blathers on, you get closer and closer. Your spider-sense is screaming—even though your eyes are shut, you know exactly where he is. But you've got to make your first strike count, because once he realizes that you're really not under his influence, there's no telling what could happen.

Make a Fighting FEAT roll. If the result is 10 or less, go to **177**. If the result is 11 or more, go to **147**.

138 Overwhelmed by Mordo's hypnosis, your mind goes entirely over into his control.

"What—do you want me to do?" you ask him.

"We wait," says Mordo patiently.

Go to **148**.

You shake your head and call out to **139**
Strange, "Sorry, Doc. Can't turn away from it, no
matter how important the other stuff is."

He folds his arms and looks at you angrily.

Make an Intuition FEAT roll. If the result is 12 or
less, go to **159**. If it's 13 or more, go to **149**.

You finger your camera, but then decide, **140**
"No. I can't waste any time when somebody's life
is at stake." And even as you think it, you're already swinging toward her.

She sees you coming her way and takes a step
back. *Great,* you think. *The* Bugle*'s got everyone
thinking I'm a cross between Mr. Hyde and the
Boston Strangler. She won't even trust someone
who's coming to save her.* But at that instant,

there's a crashing sound behind the woman from within the building.

"Jump!" you shout in midswing and, seeing no choice, she does. Just as the ceiling behind her starts to collapse, she is in midair, the street spinning dizzily below her. And then you've got her under your arm. A flawless catch. Maybe you should be working for the Mets.

"It's all right, Miss," you say. "You're safe!"

She looks down at the street below and shrieks, "Safe! A guy with a mask is swinging around three stories up on a piece of thread and I'm supposed to be safe with him?!"

"Hmph," you say as you alight on the street with her. "Some people just don't appreciate style anymore."

Add 2 Karma points for saving the frantic young woman.

Proceed to **50**.

141　　Suddenly, that little voice in your mind isn't so little anymore. It's huge, all-consuming.

Spider-Man, my friend, you're just who I've been looking for.

I—I am?

Absolutely. Someone who could understand me—and whom I could understand. Whom I see as a kindred spirit.

But—but why me?

Isn't it obvious? You're someone who has always felt that with great power comes great responsibility. Well, it says insinuatingly, *I have so much power to give. But I can't give it to just anyone. Not just any fool can be my vessel on Earth. If someone is to be the funnel for my power,*

*it must be someone who knows what's required—
how to handle himself—how to use such power
properly.*

And—that's me? It's becoming so difficult for
you to think, but the voice keeps pushing at you
to give in.

*Of course. Because you're not afraid of power.
You accept it, use it, shape it to the best ends. The
sorcerors who destroyed me—or tried to—didn't
understand. They feared my power. They
thought that I would actually try to dominate and
conquer—that no one alive could handle the
power that I had to offer. But now there's you,
Spider-Man. Peter, my friend.*

I—I don't understand, you think. *What do I
have to do? What do you want from me?*

*Why, simply give yourself over to me. I'm com-
plete now. I have power that I've drained off from
Mordo, the fool, who didn't realize my full potential. And Clea—now see? I could have drained her
completely, but I didn't. Feel the heat in me? I
have so much power stored up I'm practically
ready to explode.*

Visions of flame dance in front of you. Flames so
enticing that they look as if they're waving to you,
telling you to join them.

Give yourself over to me, the voice says. *You
mustn't fight me. That would dilute the power.
You must be willing. Let me give all the power to
you, and together we can do anything. No more
money problems. No more sickly Aunt May—how
would you like to cure her with a wave of your
hand? No more Jonah Jameson to bother you.
Everything will be perfect, just like in that dream
you had this morning. The perfect world. Just
give yourself to me, so that I can be your slave.*

119

It all sounds so tempting, so wonderful. And yet, something deep inside you shouts, *It's wrong! No one should have this much power. It'll destroy you!*

Make a Psyche FEAT roll, adding Karma if you wish. If the result is 13 or less, go to **116**. If it's 14 or more, go to **150**.

142 "Everyone calm down!" Cushing shouts. "Come on, people! It was obviously some sort of gag. Some holographic projection. We'll probably get a phone call from the 'genius' who did it, asking for a write-up."

Gradually, calm is restored, but your mind is racing. Was he looking for you? Although he never said how, Doc knows that Peter Parker is Spider-Man. Was he trying to summon you? Or maybe it was just coincidence—Doc was on his way somewhere and he happened to pass through. After all, he never looked directly at you.

"Parker!" Cushing says. "I don't know why I still have patience with you, but I have a photo assignment for you. Some baseball player is cutting a rap album and he's invited the press to send representatives. Nice, simple, quick money. Lucky for you I'm in a good mood. You want it?"

If you want to pass the assignment and go check out Doctor Strange's place to see what's up, go to **34**. If you don't want Cushing to throttle you, go to **162**.

143 "Yo! Frosty the Abominable Snowman! Get over here so I can knock the snowflakes out of you!"

The monster turns toward you and snarls, his lips drawing back to reveal yellowed teeth and blackened gums. "You haven't been flossing, have you, Seymour?" you chide.

The creature roars its fury and charges at you. But you're able to get around it with ease. Even with the harsh wind slowing you down, you can still outmaneuver this overgrown hairball.

Darting past it with your ever-trusty spider-speed, you skid across the snow and wind up next to Clea, which is where you wanted to be in the first place. You have to check on her, because if she's near death you're going to have to do something quickly. You can't just kill a few minutes waltzing around with Smokey the Polar Bear and allow Clea to freeze to death.

You check her over. Her breathing is regular, her pulse is strong. Given a couple of minutes, she'll probably come to. But it may be minutes you don't have, because lover boy is charging you again. You're in a bad position, but for what it's worth, you may add 1 Karma point to your total for your concern for Clea. The beast is almost on top of you, and you have no choice but to take him on, man-to-monster.

Go to **223**.

Summoning all your strength, you take **144** a deep breath and put everything you have against the mystical bonds that hold you in check. You grunt, your face covered with sweat under your mask. But ultimately these are mystical bonds, and nothing that you can do physically affects them. You sag against the wall, panting, frustrated and angry with yourself.

Suddenly, the air in front of you starts to ripple. You blink in surprise and confusion as a hole in the air actually begins to form. Then, stepping carefully through the rip that's materialized is a stunning platinum blonde. She's dressed in a body stocking with a purple shirt and crimson tights.

Go to **154**.

145 You take several long breaths, slowly summoning all the strength to your muscles. You pull at the bonds, but they don't give the slightest sign of breaking.

You stop, panting from the exertion, and slowly come to the realization that it's not just physical imprisonment. The bonds have a dampening effect on your mind. You're being convinced by the power of the enchantment that you simply can't break free.

You block out all thoughts of defeat, all thoughts of helplessness. You put your full energy, your full power into it and slowly feel the bonds start to give way.

"I'm not," you grunt, "going to be—kept—out of all—the fun!" And with a final effort, you snap the bonds apart. You don't hear anything or feel anything. But suddenly your hands are in front of you.

You feel the sense of lethargy drain away from you.

Add 1 Karma point to your total for summoning the strength to break your bonds.

Go to **155**.

Your leap carries you clear of the spell, **146**
and you somersault upward, clinging to the ceiling and frantically trying to come up with your next move. You quickly fire your webbing but your foe easily blocks it with one of those handy-dandy shields that he seems to pull out of nowhere.

Your eyes fall on the genuine Doc Strange, being held immobile. You realize that getting him loose would be a good move, if you can only do it before Junior here changes you into a major appliance.

At that moment, a stunningly beautiful woman appears. The fake Doc Strange is taken aback as the silver-haired figure steps through a hole that's materialized in thin air. She is clad in a body stocking, the upper half a netted purple shirt, the lower half a patterned crimson pair of tights.

Go to **156**.

Mordo doesn't even see it coming. **147**
Your fist is a blur as you swing around and knock Mordo backward. The baron flies across the room, crashing into the bookshelves. Medical texts rain down on him and he tries to pull himself together so that he can launch a mystical counter-attack.

It's a comeback you're going to see he doesn't have a chance to make. Bounding forward, you send a front snap kick into him that knocks all the air out of him, and that's a considerable amount of air. Then, grabbing him by the cape, you flip backward over his head, landing in front of him and pulling the cape completely over his head.

He's momentarily blinded and that's all you need, as you smash a roundhouse to the place under the cape where you know his head has to be.

Mordo stands there a moment, refusing to believe he's unconscious, then topples backward, hitting the floor with a crash. Cautiously, you lift up the cape to see his face clearly. He is out cold. You drop the cape back over his head.

"Not too shabby," you say. You decide that you like him this way, and in order to preserve it for posterity, you web him up with his cape remaining over his head.

Then you sit back and wait.

Go to **233**.

148 Moments later, the air in front of you ripples, and a portal opens. Through it step Doctor Strange and Clea, both of whom appear tired.

"Good evening, Doctor," Mordo says jovially. "I see you managed to free yourself—or perhaps you had some help from the lovely Clea."

"Mordo, you—" Doc begins, but then suddenly spots you and his eyes widen in surprise.

Then you launch your attack.

Make a Fighting FEAT roll. If the result is 10 or less, go to **158**. If it's 11 or more, go to **168**.

149 Something's definitely out of kilter with Doc. Sure, what you're doing is important, but the master mage shouldn't be making such a big deal about a momentary pause to nail some purse snatcher.

You're going to have to keep a close eye on this situation. Add 2 Karma points, to your total, for your canny observations, and go to **159**.

NO! you shout in your mind. *I won't let* **150** *you do it!*

Summoning all your strength, all your willpower, you break the spell and hurl the amulet away from you. It bounces across the floor and skids into the corner.

Your mind begins to clear, and you realize with a distant dread what was happening. The amulet is sentient. With power beyond imagining. It's still helpless to act on its own. It needs a host body in which to operate—and your mind, untrained in mystic discipline, was a prime target for it.

You would have been its slave, its vessel. If you had kept possession of the amulet—you don't even want to think about it.

Your breath is ragged in your chest and then, suddenly, Mordo shoves his way past you, charg-

125

ing toward the amulet.

"Mine!" he shouts. "It has to be mine!"

As depleted as you are, you still lunge forward, tackling Mordo around the legs and knocking him to the floor of the study.

"You young idiot!" he screams. Suddenly, the positions are reversed. Mordo is on top of you, his thick fingers pressing in on your throat.

"I'll kill you!" he shouts. "And then nothing will stand in the way of my possessing the amulet! No—"

"Nothing, Mordo?" says a low, familiar voice.

The grip abruptly releases from your throat. Slowly, you shake your head, sitting up, trying to clear the cobwebs from your brain. As you do, you see Doctor Strange standing in front of you.

He looks a bit disheveled, a little bit out of it. Nonetheless, you know that this is indeed the good Doctor.

You follow Strange's gaze, and see the furious Mordo, cursing and snarling behind a cage of eldritch energy.

"I finally managed to break free of his cursed spell," says Strange. "Just in time, it now appea— Clea!"

He immediately goes to the fallen woman and kneels down beside her. Always in the past, you've been impressed by Strange's utter calm. Nothing ever seemed to phase him. Yet now, as he cradles Clea's head in his lap, he appears more concerned than you've ever seen him before.

"Clea," he whispers.

Slowly she opens her eyes, licks her parched lips, and says, "Stephen—is it really you?"

"Yes, Clea," he replies, choking back the emotion in his voice and fighting to maintain his pro-

126

fessional bedside manner. "It is I. It's over, my love. Mordo is defeated, thanks to you—" and he looks to you, "—and to Spider-Man."

"Aw, pshaw," you mutter.

"You were correct about him all along, Stephen," she says. "My humblest apologies if I doubted your solidness of character and abilities, Spider-Man."

"It's the outfit I wear," you reply. "When you wear colorful tights, no one thinks you're sincere. I think I'm going to start wearing a vest over this. If you wear a vest, that just screams sincerity."

And as Doc helps Clea to her feet, he says, "I admire your character, my young friend. I am well aware of the strength of the Caputo amulet, and how it can bend minds to its will. You have always been quite the flippant one, Spider-Man—but I can tell that even you are quite shaken by what happened."

"Shaken," you say resolutely, "but not stirred."

Go to **242**.

It's got to be some sort of trick, you think **151** to yourself. *A tour group just came out of here—if someone were in trouble, surely the tour group would have heard him and helped him out. It's got to be something that the mystic defenses in the amulet are putting up—to draw me off.*

Determined not to fall into this trap, you go off in the opposite direction from the voice. As you pull farther away, and it becomes clear that you are not going to aid the person calling for help, the cries cease.

You pray you've made the right decision.

Go to **52**.

152   You slam the amulet into the imprisoning field.

The last thing you immediately recall is Doc's eyes blinking, as the field dissolves. Then, as if a circuit had just been completed, the magical energy is drawn into the amulet . . . and you.

You stagger back, your mind assaulted by images and concepts you hadn't thought possible. A million dimensions are at your fingertips, yours for the taking. And all the magic that Doctor Strange performs, the miracles that he conjures up with a mere wave of his hands you now understand. You now see how it can be done. It's all so simple!

And you hear the voice in your mind, stronger than before, seductive and tempting. *The fourth quarter,* it whispers. *Get the fourth quarter. Get the final part of the amulet, and I'll give you all the power you've ever wanted. Power that you alone could use responsibly. You don't like the world the way it is? You can reshape it in the image you wish it to be. Just like in that dream you had this morning. You can have everything you ever wanted. Make me complete—and I'll make you complete.*

And yet something deep inside you shouts, *It's wrong! No one should have that kind of power! It's using you, fathead. Get rid of it. Get rid of it before it's too late!*

Make a Psyche FEAT roll, adding Karma if you wish. If the result is 12 or less, go to **172**. If the result is 13 or more, go to **62**.

153   You shrug. There were emergencies long before you were Spider-Man, and they'll crop up long after you're sick of putting on the blue and red tights.

With one vault, you leap back across the room, landing on the bed, and at that moment there is a loud pounding on your door. You and MJ glance at each other and sigh. Going to the closet and pulling on a robe, you shout, "Who is it?"

"Candi, Randi and Bambi," a female voice shouts back through the door. "Peter, there's a big emergency! Have you heard?"

You open the door reluctantly and the three neighbors from next door rush in. Bambi is in the lead and she says hurriedly, "We were sunbathing on the roof——"

"What else is new?" you sigh. On several occasions it's been that sunbathing next to your skylight exit that has impeded your comings and goings as Spider-Man.

"No, there was this huge fire!"

"On the roof?"

"No! About ten blocks away. Couldn't see much, but it looked like a mess. And traffic is all snarled up—the police and firemen can't get to it."

"You think we should evacuate?" Randi asks. "I mean, it's ten blocks away, but—"

"Okay, look," you say. "I'm a photographer with the *Daily Bugle*. I'll get over there on foot, and check it out. If the firefighters, when they get there, tell me it's really serious, I'll high-tail it back here. How's that?" They all nod, pleased that you've agreed to take a hand in this, and you realize you should have really done so in the first place. Ignoring a direct threat out of personal interest was what led to your Uncle Ben being killed those many years ago. Deduct 1 Karma point from your total.

129

You shuffle the women out, change into your Spidey threads and get up to the roof. You quickly confirm what they were saying—traffic is completely snarled.

Smoke is wafting into the air ten blocks away. You immediately swing off in that direction, eating up distance in seconds.

Go to **30**.

154 She approaches you quickly, saying, "I've come to get you out. We haven't much time—he could detect my presence at any moment."

"Uh—right."

You're not exactly in a position to trust her, but do you have much choice?

To take your chances with her, go to **174**. To tell her to buzz off, go to **164**.

155 Silently, you push open the door, and look up at the maze of stairs that leads upward.

From somewhere far above you, you hear a deep, gutteral voice uttering chants you suspect you were never meant to hear. What's that line from *MacBeth?* "Screw your courage to the sticking place." Well, your courage is about as screwed and stuck as it's going to be.

You start to climb upward, not stepping on the stairs, but preferring to climb along the walls. You make your way aimlessly for seemingly endless moments, unsure of where you're going or even if you should be going. Then, as you crawl past one juncture of the stairs, you see light gleaming through the top of a door at the head of the stairs.

And from there you can hear that awful voice now laughing in satisfaction. *One thing's for sure—that's definitely not Doc's voice.*

As you carefully make your way toward the door, you think to yourself, *Maybe Doc's been possessed or something. But who could have taken him over? Could it be . . . ?*

You shake your head. You've been watching too much late-night television.

You get to the top of the stairs and peer in, freezing in shock.

Doc Strange is beside himself—literally. One Doc stands there, speaking in the weird voice you heard earlier. In his right hand he holds the three-

quarters amulet you recovered. In his left he holds the other quarter, and he's about to insert it into the rest.

The other Doctor Strange—the one floating in the middle of the Sanctum Sanctorum, bereft of his cloak and other mystic talismans—stares straight ahead, helplessly.

"I've waited a long time for you to see this moment, Strange. The moment when I become the true sorceror supreme on this planet," the imposter says.

By the way he's holding the amulet, you might have a clear shot at it with your webbing. Then again, you might miss it and make him mad.

Do you try to snag the amulet with webbing (**26**), or do you opt for the better part of valor, and split (**16**)?

156   The silver-haired woman calls out in a furious tone, "How dare you wear Stephen's form?"

The imposter spins and shouts, "You!"

"You're finished, monster," she snaps, drawing her arms up.

It's clear to you what her first move is going to be. Unfortunately, while it's clear to you, it's clear to the fake Doc Strange as well. He quickly gestures, muttering an incantation you couldn't repeat for a million bucks, and the unmoving form of the real Doc Strange vanishes.

"How dare you!" she screams.

He grins maliciously. "One who wields the Caputo amulet dares anything. And the moment I join its pieces together as a whole, I shall—"

Quickly, you grab one of Doc's many mystic

tomes, and hurl the book at the fake mage. It knocks the amulet from his outstretched hand. The amulet clatters to the floor, mere feet away from him.

"Hah!" shouts the woman, immediately launching a mystic assault. The Sanctum is alive with corruscating colors.

There are two approaches you can take. You can join the young woman in her frontal assault on this carbon copy Doc (**94**), or you can try to grab the amulet that is sitting so invitingly on the floor just out of his reach (**15**).

Almost out of nowhere, a huge, white, **157** hairy creature that kind of reminds you of the Wendigo leaps into view. Its body is covered with coarse, matted white fur. The wind shifts and you catch a whiff—it's not pretty.

The creature is standing right over Clea, and before you can move, he swings a massive clawed hand at her, knocking her back to the ground. He looms over her, roaring into the wind.

What in the name of Santa is it? Another Wendigo? An abominable snowman? That would certainly support Clea's contention that you're in the Himalayas.

It doesn't matter. All that does matter is that you act quickly, or Clea could wind up as bloody ribbons in the snow.

The amulet is sitting in the snow, possibly with enough power to wipe this creature out—if it's somehow magically based. And over there is Doc Strange, the guy who could clear up this mess with a wave of his hand. But by the time you got over to him, Clea could be dead. And it's possible

134

that she's already dying. If you don't cover her in webbing or something for insulation, she could die of exposure.

Do you make helping Clea your top priority (**143**), make a move to grab the amulet (**133**), or try to slug it out with the monster (**223**)?

Your attack has the advantage of sur- **158** prise, but because Mordo has command over your mind, you're moving much more slowly than you ordinarily would. As a result, Doctor Strange is able to react in time—except that he doesn't block with a mystical attack. It's almost as if he's conserving energy, as he turns quickly and, catching your outstretched arm, hurls you in a perfect judo throw.

Your reflexes are still fast enough that you land on your feet. Then, from a crouched position, you see Mordo come up behind the still woozy Clea. Her costume is covered with snow and frost and there's a claw mark on her arm—wherever she came from getting Doc, she didn't have an easy time of it.

Mordo strikes, hitting Clea from behind. She drops to her knees and the amulet flies out of her hand.

Mordo starts to reach for the amulet, grinning, evilly triumphant. And from across the room Doc is calling, "Spider-Man! Concentrate! You must break free from Mordo's influence! Stop him before it's too late!"

There's a pounding in your head, and you feel as if you're being ripped in two directions at the same time.

Go to **188**.

159 "Just cool your jets, Doc, I'll be right back," you say, and before he can scowl at you further you swing down toward the fleeing thief.

This is a piece of cake. The kid glances behind himself to see if he's being pursued, and the next thing he knows he runs straight into a large glob of extra-sticky webbing you've left hanging in his path.

Huffing and puffing, the woman arrives behind the boy and looks at him sternly as you swing away. Add 1 Karma point to your total, for your civic-mindedness.

Go to **169**.

160 Anticipating Dagger's attack, you leap. She hurls her light daggers but you somersault over them, spinning perfectly and landing on the wall behind her.

She turns, in that graceful, dancer's manner she has—it's not a turn as much as a pirouette. Quickly, you bring your webbing into play.

Make an Agility with Webbing FEAT roll. If the result is 18 or less, go to **22**. If the result is 19 or more, go to **170**.

161 You lapse into unconsciousness, as the bobbies pile on top of you. When you wake up, you find yourself a prisoner in a British jail, accused of resisting arrest, causing a ruckus, and dressing in a silly costume.

Immediately, you start to lodge a protest and are told that your lawyer will be with you shortly. At which point, the entire world suddenly goes up in flames.

"Um . . . sure," you say. There's no way **162** you can pass up the bucks. You have a wife to consider now, not just your career as a web-swinging wonder.

You get the address from Kate Cushing, go downstairs . . . and suddenly realize that you can't shirk your responsibility as Spider-Man. Doctor Strange wouldn't just come floating through unless there were a good reason for it. Before you do anything, you have to check out what's going on at Doc Strange's house.

Reluctantly, you go back up to the *Bugle* city room and track down Cushing. She looks at you ominously. "What is it, Parker?"

"Look, Kathy . . . Kate . . . Katey . . . something's come up. There's no way that I can do this assignment. Something really unexpected has—"

She puts up a hand and, frighteningly, smiles. "Now, Peter . . . there's no problem."

"There's not?"

"No. I can always get another photographer."

"But Katey . . . Kate . . . Kathy—"

"Miss Cushing," she corrects icily. "You took an assignment from me and then backed out. I need someone to count on. Good day, Mister Parker."

You sigh and walk out. This has not been your day. You hope that whatever's going on with Doc, it's something major league. You'll need something major to distract you from the fiasco this day has been.

Unwisely, you forget about the old Chinese proverb—don't make wishes lightly, or you may get them.

You head up to the roof of the*Daily Bugle* and seconds later are webbing downtown as Spidey.

Go to **80**.

163   "Hey, okay, Doc," you say. "There's no need to get crazy about it. Here."

You toss the amulet to Doc Strange and as he catches it, an inhuman glow lights up his face.

Go to **118**.

164   "Forget it," you reply. "This is another stupid trick. I've been played for a sucker three times already—four if you count my getting stuck in here. There's no way I'm going to get burned again."

She stares at you in annoyance. "I don't have time to waste with you. If you don't want to help me, I'll do it myself."

"Fine."

"Fine. You can stay down here until you rot."

The woman—your last chance of getting out of this place alive—steps back into the hole in the air and vanishes.

"Hah!" you say. "I showed her." But her words come true. You *do* end up staying here until you rot.

165 You try to leap out of the way, but, as if they had eyes, Dagger's light weapons cut through the air and slam through you, sending you down, clutching at the non-existent wound in your chest.

The world spins around you and, in the distance, you hear Dagger say, "But Cloak! He's not evil!"

"He attacked you," Cloak intones. "Perhaps he is evil, perhaps he's not—but no one attacks you with impunity."

Then darkness swallows you up.

Go to **176**.

166 *Good time to take the bull by the horns,* you think, leaping full steam at Mordo, holding the treasured amulet in front of you. With the adhering power of your fingers, nothing is going to be able to rip it from your grasp.

The mystic villain sees you coming and launches arcane, black magic at you. Your radioactive blood freezes as his assault leaps across the room. The amulet burns hot in your hand. You gasp at the heat, then, like a small vacuum cleaner, the amulet draws all the power of the spell into itself.

"Curse you!" he shouts.

"*Gesundheit,*" you reply, getting ready to take a swing at him. Abruptly, he spits out a spell. You brace yourself, waiting for another assault, but he vanishes, along with the immobile Doctor Strange. And even as he does so, his voice seems to fill the air, "You've only won a temporary respite, Spider-Man. My demons will track you down, wherever you hide. You're a dead man, Spider-Man. You just don't know it yet."

With those cheerful words ringing in your ears, you leap up to Doc's ornate skylight, open it, and swing out into the night.

Go to **78**.

"Better take a minute or two to see what **167** I've got here, options-wise," you say, and with one powerful leap you land on the wall of the nearby building.

Clinging there, you look up and wait to see if Cloak is pursuing you. Instead, he remains where he is, looking menacing. The shadow reaches down to where you had been, then withdraws.

"What's the matter, Cloak? you call. "Having eclipse problems?"

"Do not mock me, Spider-Man," says Cloak warningly. "I can assure you that you will not live to regret it."

"Ooooh, I'm so scared," you say, as you quickly race through your options.

The shadow has crept back all right, but not all that far. If you try to scale the building again, it will overwhelm you in no time. There's a window, though, that someone of your agility can easily leap through, even from where you are now. The other option, of course, is to drop to the ground and go through the front door.

If you want to spring through the window, go to **238**. If, however, you want to try the front door, go to **226**.

You lunge forward. Doc attempts to **168** ward you off, but it's clear that he needs, at the very least, a few seconds to pull himself together after this latest jaunt—a few seconds you simply will not allow.

You slam into Doc, knocking him back. He manages to cushion the blow somewhat but is momentarily stunned by the fierceness of your attack.

You turn to find Clea suddenly there. Her costume is covered with snow and frost, and there's what appears to be a rip in her skin made by a claw. By rights, she should be just as knocked out as Doc, on her last legs physically and psychically. But seeing you attack Doctor Strange just then, seeing you ruthlessly knock him across the room, has unleashed new reserves in her, fired her anger beyond the point where she will acknowledge defeat.

She raises a hand at point-blank range and a spell carries you back. You have lost control of the situation—you can't think fast enough to react to anything because Mordo still has a clamp on your mind. Part of you doesn't want to react, doesn't want to battle Strange and Clea.

You hit the floor, and despite yourself you start to get to your feet. You turn and see that Doc has recovered, and now he's gesturing toward you . . .

Then everything goes black.

Go to **178**.

169   You swing off after the floating figure of Doc Strange as he glides silently toward the Casbah. Then you lose sight of him.

Oh great, you think to yourself, as you land on top of the wall surrounding the Casbah. *What am I supposed to do now? Go to Traveler's Aid and ask them to steer me toward a missing quarter of the Caputo amulet?*"

Then you see Doc again, floating near a tall, narrow tower at the far end of the Casbah. There are several smaller buildings nearby, but the tower definitely dominates. It's about six stories tall,

narrow, like a giant needle pointing the way toward the stars. The exterior appears to be hardened clay, and the roof flares out at the top like a mushroom.

You swing over there, watching carefully, wondering just what's going to be tossed at you. If the amulet quarter is hidden in that tower, then you can expect to be facing somebody shortly who you would rather not encounter. Who will it be? Electro? Doc Ock? The Sin-Eater? Gee, the things you have to look forward to.

Go to **179**.

170

Your web shot is perfect, catching Dagger in midair and snagging her around the legs. With a shocked squeal, she pitches forward, her chin connecting with the hard clay floor. You don't hesitate. Taking the opportunity, you dash to a set of spiral stairs against the far wall.

"Come back here, Spider-Man! I have to stop you!" calls Dagger, but by this time you've already started up the stairs, out of her range.

Go to **209**.

171 You feint, then try to come in with an uppercut. But all the wind and blowing snow throws off your spider-sense. Then you slip on the uncertain ground. Give you something clean to adhere to—a wall, pavement—and you're absolutely unmoveable, but something covered with oil or water, and its just as difficult for you to hold onto as for anyone else.

And as you try to get yourself back on track, the creature swings his arm around with a devastating round-house punch. There's no art, no form, no style in it, but plenty of strength as he connects, hurling you across the snow.

You roll over, and crash into a formation of rocks. (Reduce your Health score by 8 points.)

If the frozen air is still going in and out of your lungs, go to **81**.

144

"Perfect, yes," you say, and your mind **172** begins to glaze over.

But from behind you, a deep, powerful voice says, "No! You shall not have him!" You turn to see Doctor Strange facing you. His hands up, his mouth murmuring incantations, he's immediately launching an attack on you.

Stop him! screams the voice in your mind. *I'm not ready yet! Stop him!!* You leap toward Doctor Strange—

And everything goes black.

Go to **28**.

"Sorry, Doc," you say, slowly backing **173** away, "but I'm getting the feeling that giving you this thing could be hazardous to my health."

Strange's face becomes taut and set. There is almost no trace of the calm, confident magician you've come to know. He's absolutely livid.

"You fool! You've brought this on yourself." Bolts of magical energy leap all around you.

Go to **208**.

"All right," you say, shrugging. **174** "What've I got to lose? If I don't trust you, I could probably wind up sitting here until I rot."

She makes a simple pass of her hand and the bonds holding you vanish. "Could you teach me that?" you ask.

"You cold have done it yourself," she replies, "if you had greater belief in yourself."

"Hey, I'm pure of heart. You can't get much better than that."

She sighs in exasperation and says, "Come on.

Now is our chance to get out of here and get the amulet."

Go to **183**.

175 Taking aim, you fire a webline that snags the larger piece of the amulet in Doc's hand. He turns in alarm, sputtering as you yank the amulet out of his hand. In a split second it's nestled neatly in your grasp. And incredibly, you hear a small voice in the back of your head, saying, *You got here just in time.*

You find yourself faced with an angry magician, who turns on you with a face as dark as storm clouds and a disposition worse than the Boston Strangler's.

"Put it down, you young fool," he snarls. "You have no idea of the amount of power you're toying with. It could destroy you where you stand. Give it to me before you put an end to everything!"

Do you fight him (**166**), or get while the getting's good (**68**)?

You are reduced to a gibbering wreck, **176** and your adventure is over.

You hesitate just a moment, making **177** sure that you know just where Mordo is, and then you let fly with a left to the jaw.

But something in your posture, something in the way you approached him, warned Mordo at the last moment. He reacts barely quickly enough to roll with the punch, stopping several feet away. He is rattled but still very conscious and very, very dangerous.

With all the mystic transporting and hopping around and fighting spells he's been doing, Mordo is extremely tired. But that doesn't stop him from launching a potentially deadly blast of energy.

Make an Agility FEAT roll. If the result is 13 or less, go to **197**. If it is 14 or more, go to **187**.

178   You barely manage to open your eyes.

Doc is staring down at you. "Are you all right, Spider-Man?"

You moan low in your throat, "My head feels like it's been used for place kicking practice. What happened?"

"Mordo," Strange says evenly. "But it's all right. I was able to defeat you—and him. He was at the end of his strength, mystically speaking. And you didn't have your heart in the fight. It was not difficult."

"So the world's safe for democracy and apple pie?"

Clea walks up and stands next to Strange, resting her hand lightly on his shoulder. "You were right, Spider-Man," she says. "Mordo was here. If I'd listened to you I might have been here to help you."

"Or Mordo might have beaten the two of us and won everything. You never know."

You lean back and let the darkness take you. You'll sleep for the next five hours and then, eventually, you'll head home—chagrined that Doctor Strange had to save your hash this time around. On the other hand, at least you're still in one piece. And as they say in flight school, any landing you walk away from is a good one.

179   You stand outside the tower, tilting back on your heels and staring straight up. Your spider-sense is already buzzing—the whole shebang is filled with danger, just lurking inside.

"They don't pay me enough for this," you mutter.

You wonder what your best approach would be.

There is a large wooden door at the base of the tower. It's covered with dirt and cobwebs—obviously this place hasn't been entered in ages. The side of the tower, by the same token, is grimey but easily climbable.

If you want to go in through the door, go to **214**. If, however, you decide to crawl up the exterior of the building, go to **189**.

You can see the confident, complacent **180** look on Cloak's face. The last thing he's expecting is a direct assault. You leap at him, firing your webbing.

For a moment, surprise flickers over Cloak's face, but he recovers far too quickly. He spreads his arms as if welcoming you, and moments later you are enveloped in darkness.

Go to **237**.

"Hold the phone, Doc," you say to the **181** floating apparition. "I've gone along with this up until now, but no more."

You see by his expression that he was not expecting this response from you, but you've gone this far.

"All this stuff fighting guys who are taken from my mind, guys who aren't really here—that's not my usual thing. Costumed clowns, crazed burglars, those guys—that's my bread and butter."

You reach into your belt and extract the fragments of the amulet that you've collected.

"Here," you say. "Take what I've got and get somebody else. Call Doctor Druid, Doctor Spock—anybody. But this is way out of my league. Get me out of here."

Go to **191**.

You look around and come to the conclu- **182** sion, within two seconds, that there is no other way.

Go to **220**.

She makes another gesture and the door **183** to the room swings open.

"After you," you say, bowing galantly.

The two of you go up the stairs. The woman walks so quietly that she makes no sound at all. Then you realize that she's not really stepping on the stairs, but literally walking on air, her feet about a half-inch above the actual steps.

Of course, you're no slouch either when it comes to stealth. You creep up the wall, avoiding the stairs altogether.

From ahead you hear a low, strangely accented voice making unpleasant-sounding incantations. You want to ask this charming, if somewhat bizarre, woman just what the devil's going on, but you don't want to risk being heard.

You weave in and out of several side entrances and eventually find yourself approaching the top of the stairs, with the woman at your side.

There's a light at the top of the stairs. You poke your head through the doorway there, and what you see chills your body. Doc Strange is there, all right—twice.

One of them floats there in what appears to be some sort of suspended animation, surrounded by a faintly glowing field of power. His cape and that fancy brooch he always wears around his neck are gone, and he's staring straight up. You don't think he's dead—but he's sure seen better days.

And standing over him is the other Doc Strange—the one who had been trying to turn you into bacon bits. In his right hand is the three-quarters amulet that you managed to acquire, and in his left is the remaining quarter.

"Watch helplessly, Strange!" he says in that same, deep voice you heard moments earlier. "Watch as I put the final segment into the Caputo amulet, and become the master mage in all the dimensions."

Bummer, you think.

Go to **156**.

184 *She's not budging an inch,* you think. *This is a golden opportunity—and I'm not gonna waste it.*

Go to **219**.

You blink in surprise. "Did you do that?" **185** you ask.

The woman's mouth twitches in annoyance. "No," she replies angrily. "He vanished of his own accord—and he took Stephen with him."

"You know Doc?"

She glances at you. "Intimately. Stephen Strange sent me to find you. Come, we've much to discuss." She floats up toward the skylight with its elaborate design etched on it, and it obediently swings up and back as she gracefully arcs out into the night sky.

Well, you sure don't know what to make of this, but you don't see a whole lot of choices. You follow her out into the evening air and look for a rooftop where the two of you can settle down and talk.

Go to **110**.

186   You hate to admit it, but she really does have a point. There's really no reason that Mordo would want to head right back with Doc to the house—not with the entire world, not to mention countless dimensions, to hide out in.

Go to **103**.

187   You leap over the bolt of energy and, somersaulting in midair, land with your feet in Mordo's face. He goes down and this time he's not getting up.

Quickly, you web up his mouth so that he can't start making any new and exciting incantations to drive you crazy, then carefully and methodically web him from head to toe.

"There," you say with satisfaction. "All nice and gift wrapped." Then you sit down and wait.

Go to **233**.

188   Make a Psyche FEAT roll, adding Karma if you wish. If the result is 12 or less go to **98**. If it's 13 or more, go to **19**.

189   *Most people would enter through the door,* you reason. *Being Spider-Man means I don't have to be like most people.*

One leap carries you up onto the side of the building. You cling there for a moment, assessing your situation, then you start to climb up the side.

Your spider-sense buzzes more strongly now, but you don't see an immediate threat. Then again, just because you don't see it doesn't mean it's not coming. The question is, where will it come from?

Suddenly, you look. Standing on the top of the tower is Cloak—one-half of Cloak and Dagger!

But they're not bad guys, you think to yourself—except, when you first met them, they were your opponents. Cloak and Dagger, two teen-aged runaways who became the victims of bizarre body-altering drugs.

Cloak, a young man, was made into a living shadow. Within the folds of his massive cloak were all the nightmares one would never hope to encounter. As for his beautiful accomplice, Dagger—

You realize you don't have time to think about her, as Cloak, several stories above you at the top of the tower, suddenly spreads wide his all-enfolding cloak.

"You've made a great mistake coming here, Spider-Man," he says in that beyond-the-grave voice of his. "Apparently, I must teach you the errors of your ways."

"Oh, good," you say with a joviality you don't feel. "I'm such a slow learner."

Blackness emerges from within the dark emptiness of Cloak's body. It starts down the tower toward you like something alive. *This is definitely not a great situation to be in,* you think.

Perched on the wall, you see a window next to you. But your spider-sense is tingling—there's danger in there, too. Then again, there's plenty of danger out here.

To try attacking Cloak, go to **180**. To leap through the window into the building, go to **238**. If, however, you want to jump to the adjacent building and reassess your options, go to **167**.

190 You ricochet around the confined area like a pinball. Dagger hurls her light daggers but they miss you entirely—and nail Cloak.

All the menace vanishes from his face and a sigh escapes his lips. Then you remember—Cloak's darkness almost has a life of its own, with an insatiable appetite for light. The only thing that can momentarily still his creeping darkness is the living light of Dagger.

Grabbing the opportunity, you bound over Cloak, who is blocking your way. Keeping him between you and Dagger, you've gotten the seconds you need as you charge up the stairs.

Go to **121**.

191 There is an all-enveloping burst of light and you cover your eyes to shield your face.

"Doc!" you shout. "You don't have to take it personally!"

Suddenly you are surrounded by darkness. There's only the faintest glimmering of light, just enough to enable you to see a tall dark form standing in front of you.

"Doc?" you whisper, and your spider-sense starts to buzz.

Go to **204**.

192 The last thing Mordo would expect is a frontal assault. It would be an incredibly stupid, foolhardy thing to do. But doing the expected isn't how you manage to keep your head on your shoulders. You leap directly at Mordo.

Alarmed by the immediate physical menace, Mordo steps back and quickly gestures, muttering a few more of those names of people that you're really glad you won't have to meet.

And suddenly huge winds come out of nowhere, buffeting you backward.

"Try the Winds of Watoomb, you webbed fool!" shouts Mordo." They're summoned from another dimension, and even the cursed amulet can't absorb them because they're not a direct spell. Oh, the most novice of novices could use the amulet's power to counter it—but you don't have that knowledge, do you?"

"Is that a rhetorical question?" you shout as you try to bring the amulet around, but the winds are all around you. They want to pick you up, hurl you with all their power against a wall and reduce you to a bloodied pulp.

But even the Winds of Wahoo, or whatever he called it, have to contend with the awesome adhesion power of your feet and hands. You keep your feet braced on the floor, concentrating on maintaining the bond with the hardwood beneath you. You issue a prayer of thanks to the gods of superheroes that you weren't standing on a throw rug or something when this started—you would have looked pretty silly smeared all over the wall with a rug attached to your feet.

"Give it back, Spider-Man!" shouts Mordo. "Let go of the amulet and you'll be permitted to leave!"

"That's—awfully decent of you!" you shout back. These are more than just pure winds— they're scrambling your thoughts, making it hard for you to think. But you've got to get to Mordo.

Make a combined Endurance and Fighting FEAT roll, adding Karma if you wish. If the result is 17 or less, go to **123**. If the result is 18 or more, go to **13**.

193 You don't have time to think. All you can do is rely on your spider-sense, which is seeming to tell you that Doc Strange is, at this moment, a full-blown menace.

You leap directly at Doc, one fist pulled back. Maybe what this mystic muddle needs is some good old-fashioned physical solutions. And you're just the webhead to provide them.

Go to **14**.

194 Seymour shakes to the right and left to hurl you off. You hear his labored breathing and, giving it everything you've got, increase the pressure even more.

Now Seymour claws desperately at you. The claws, flailing wildly, glance off your arm, scratching you. They don't do you any serious damage, but you grit your teeth against the pain, and press even harder.

"Fall, blast it!" you shout over the wind. "Fall! Fall! Fall!"

Then the creature finally topples forward, his body going limp. You ride him down, shouting, "Timber!" and Seymour lands with a crash, sending up an explosion of snow.

You stay there for long seconds, making sure that the great beast isn't faking it. But there is no motion from him, no movement whatsoever, and slowly you release your hold.

You stagger shakily to your feet and rasp out, "Piece—of cake."

You suck in lungfuls of air, and gain 1 Karma point for your triumph. Now you must to tend to Clea—and pray you're not too late.

Go to **221**.

The blackness holds you prisoner. If you **195** don't break free soon, you never will.

Make a combined Psyche and Endurance FEAT roll, adding Karma if you wish. If the result is 20 or less, go to **176**. If it's 21 or more, go to **206**.

Your adventure has just been derailed. **196**

You try desperately to leap clear of it, but **197** the mystic bolt tracks you as if it had eyes. It feels like being slammed into by a small tank, as you are hurled back by the force of it. Jeez, if this is a weak mystic bolt, you'd hate to think what one at full force would be like.

And as you lie there, trying to sort out your completely scrambled brains, Mordo is suddenly above you.

"Now, Spider-Man," he says evilly, "you will serve me. And this time you don't have the will-power to resist."

And he's right.

Go to **138**.

Summoning every ounce of energy you **198** have, you send a roundhouse punch smashing into the creature's face. The power of it knocks Seymour off his feet. The winds, so hostile to you before, seem to act in your favor now as they practically pick the creature up, sending him flying across the snow.

When he lands, he skids farther and farther back, out of control on the snow and ice—and vanishes.

You blink, confused. *Where did he go?*

You follow his trajectory, looking at the skid marks, hoping he's not just hiding and planning to leap out at you.

Then suddenly, your spider-sense does start to buzz but not because of Seymour. You stop in your tracks and peer forward carefully.

Directly in front of you is a sheer drop—the edge of an enormous cliff. Carefully, you peer over and see nothing. The snow is whirling and whipping around, giving you no indication of just how far or how deep Seymour may have fallen.

You shake your head. Despite the fact that it tried to kill you, you find yourself hoping it's okay. Just so it stays out of your hair, so you can do what you have to and get out of here.

Go to **221**.

The world is wrenched around you once **199**
more and you think to yourself, *Well, at least this
is the last time I have to feel like I was just tossed
into a blender.*

You land, this time in familiar surroundings.
Doc's reception room, where all of this craziness
first started. You stop a moment to get your bear-
ings, wavering slightly in place.

Doc hovers there in a lotus position, staring
blankly at nothing. You take a step forward,
frowning, snapping your fingers. "Doc?"

Then Strange's ectoplasmic form glides
through the wall and rejoins with his physical
form. You kick yourself mentally. Of course he
couldn't respond—he quite literally wasn't home.

Life returns to his empty eyes, and he smiles at
you. You realize, with some surprise, just how
rare it is for Doc to actually smile.

"It is good to see you hale and hearty, my
friend," he says. "Now, if you don't mind—please
hand the amulet to me." You stare down at the
warm three-quarters circle of stone in your hand.

If you hand it to him, go to **8**. If you want to hold
off giving it to him, go to **23**.

"Now," says Clea imperiously, "we must **200**
make something understood from the beginning."

"Well, I just hope that doesn't confuse anyone
who might be coming in late," you reply.

She stares at you. "Oh—yes," she says. "Humor. I think that humor is not appropriate at this
time."

"Not appropriate! Look, lady," you say, starting
to feel a little annoyed with her high-faluting man-

ner, "I know you're concerned about Doc. I know you're a hot-shot dimension hopper and I'm a measely little costumed hotdog. But at this point, I've been in three major cities in less than an hour, fought simulations of some of my toughest enemies plucked out of my own mind, then some guy powerful enough to lay out Doctor Strange tries to turn me into a toaster or something. There are some things that we simple-minded, humble mortals have to joke about. Otherwise we'd go stark-raving mad."

"Spider-Man," she says, trying to hide the fact that you are clearly straining her patience, which naturally puts you more in a mood to puncture her bubble of pretentiousness, "Stephen has spoken in the past, very highly of you. For that reason, I am willing to include you in the rest of this—problem. But we are dealing with forces and realms that you cannot even begin to understand. Your mind is undisciplined, and, unless you keep your wits about you, you could easily become a liability. In my realm, I am the ruler. I am the liberator. Now," and she extends her hand, "give me the amulet and we'll be on our way to find Stephen."

Your spider-sense isn't tingling in the slightest. You're absolutely positive that she is who she says she is. But you're not so sure that you want to play it exactly her way.

If you decide to go along with her to rescue Doc, and try to put aside your differences, then go to **103**. If you decide to just give her the amulet and tell her to take a hike, then go to **128**. Or maybe you should go back to Strange's house and snoop around there some more to see what you can find (**239**).

162

You're crawling around in the Coliseum, **201** looking for some sign of which way to go, when you see Doc floating about twenty yards away.

"Hey Doc!" you shout. "Don't just make like Casper the Friendly Ghost. Help me out here, will ya?"

As if in answer, Doc floats toward the middle of the arena of the Coliseum.

"Help!!"

Under your mask, you blink. Was that Doc screaming for help? No, of course not—when Doc's ectoplasmic form speaks, you hear it in your mind, not with your ears. And this was most definitely out loud.

If you want to check out the source of the cry, go to **122**. If you want to head straight for the center of the coliseum, go to **151**.

202 "Spidey express, comin' atcha!" you shout, as you spring at Hobgoblin. He pulls a pumpkin bomb out of his weapons bag, but you're already high in the air, kicking it out of his grasp. It falls to the ground, and explodes harmlessly some feet away.

But the Hobgoblin has managed to grab you by the ankle, and his strength is overwhelming. The two of you tumble backward in the air, struggling furiously. He spits out his anger and hatred of you and together you hit the train track.

Beneath you, the ground rumbles, and you realize that a train is rolling your way.

Make an Agility FEAT roll, adding Karma if you wish. If the result is 12 or less, go to **196**. If it's 13 or more, go to **37**.

Laying her down gently, you say, "Stay **203** put, honey. This'll only take a minute."

You easily leap over the Rhino's head, grabbing his horn and spinning him around and off course.

"You got a death wish?" shouts the Rhino.

"Oh yeah," you reply. *"Death Wish, Mister Majestyk—all those Bronson films, all on tape."*

The Rhino charges you and you spend your time simply staying out of his way. The Rhino's big and powerful, but he's not long on brains.

He charges left and right as you use your speed and agility to stay one step ahead of him. "Stop dancing around!" shouts the Rhino, and you hear his breath rasping in his chest.

"What? And give up my reputation as the Baryshnikov of super-guys?"

You come to a halt directly beneath the emperor's box. Many feet above you, the emperor puts his hand straight out, and then points his thumb down. "I like you, too!" you shout in response to the death sentence the emperor has just pronounced for you.

The Rhino charges you once again. He's considerably slower than he was before. Your bouncing around wore him down somewhat. But he's still dangerous.

Now, though, you're in the perfect position to execute your plan—provided you've still got the strength to do it.

Make a Strength FEAT roll, adding Karma before you roll if you wish. If the result is 10 or less, go to **218**. If it is 11 or more, go to **33**.

"No," he rumbles in a heavily accented **204** voice. "No, not Doc. Not at all."

You hold the amulet pieces in your hand and he gestures. Suddenly, your hand is empty and he is holding the partially assembled amulet.

"Even partially assembled," he rumbles, "the amulet will provide me with overwhelming power. You have done me some service, Spider-Man, however pitiful. I will not kill you."

You leap toward him he's not there.

Actually, you're not there. Suddenly, the world is white, and a harsh wind cuts through the thin fabric of your costume. You look around and discover that you're in some sort of vast, white wasteland.

The Arctic? The Antarctic? Ultimately, it doesn't matter. Wherever you are, it's sure not close enough to whoever sent you here to make any difference.

"All right," you shout to no one in particular. "It's pretty obvious I was suckered. But you made one mistake, buddy boy—you left me alive. And while I'm alive, I'll come back. And I'll find out what happened—and I'll make you sorry you messed with me."

And you probably will. But for now your adventure is over.

You may, of course, start again. Start out with 1 less Karma point of your initial score, however, because of what you already know.

You turn away from the encroaching **205** shadow on the stairway above and head back down. Dagger is standing there, waiting for you.

You pause, trying to sort out your next move. To your surprise, Dagger isn't moving either.

Go to **222**.

Surrounded by darkness, you stagger to **206** your feet.

"No," you shout. "I won't be a prisoner in my own skull!"

Somewhere in the distance, you hear Cloak's voice saying "Dagger! He's too strong! I can't hold him!"

You put everything you've got into it, swinging at the darkness as if it were tangible—and suddenly you're out in the light.

The light never looked as good to you as you lunge away from Cloak's dark embrace. Dizzy, confused, you tumble down the spiral stairs. After a moment of thudding down the steps, you stop rolling forward with a desperate grab of your hand.

You look up, your head spinning.

Dagger stands there in front of you, her hands spread, ready to hurl more light daggers.

Do you immediately leap to the attack (**219**), or do you wait for Dagger to make the first move (**222**)?

207 You swing through the city, the amulet now webbed to your forearm just in case you need it. *But—need it for what?* you wonder. Somewhere in the back of your mind, it seems to whisper, *Power. Power* . . . It falls silent again, and you pull up short with a yell.

Floating directly in front of you is one of Mordo's ghostly agents, reaching out toward you. You backflip and land on a wall, clinging there for a moment. Do you attack this bizarre ghostly image (**10**), or run as if the devil is on your tail (which it very well might be (**89**))?

208 Make an Intuition FEAT roll, adding Karma if you wish. If the result is 14 or less, go to **193**. If it's 15 or more, go to **114**.

209 You bound up the steps, bouncing off the walls for further speed, and suddenly your spider-sense goes berserk. There's danger in front of you—and you can guess what that is. There's also danger behind you—and you *know* who that is.

Do you go forward, taking your chances with whatever's ahead (**216**), or go back and face the beautiful but deadly Dagger (**205**)?

210 *The first thing to do is make sure he doesn't have a prayer of assembling the whole*

169

amulet, you think to yourself. *Best way to ensure that, is if I have all four pieces.*

Make an Agility with Webbing FEAT roll, adding Karma if you wish. If the result is 20 or less, go to **132**. If it's 21 or more, go to **229**.

211   You pull your fist back and, focusing everything you have into this punch, let fly with a roundhouse that you could swear would stop a rhino in its tracks. It knocks the creature back, but he gets up so quickly that you realize you didn't quite connect fully.

You try to move out of the way of the creature's attack but he lunges forward and swings. You manage to roll with the punch to some degree, but it's not enough to prevent you from skidding across the snow like a hockey puck.

You blink, trying to stop the world from spinning around you, and you try to pull yourself together enough to get back into this fight.

Go to **81**.

212   You wait for Dagger to press the attack, but she hesitates, too. It gives you the time you need for your stamina and endurance to kick in. Slowly, even though your body tells you that you should just curl up and die, you fight off the numbing paralysis.

"Spider-Man," she starts to say, when suddenly, blindly, you spray your webbing, hoping to buy yourself some time. You hear an "ooof" that indicates you have managed to slow her down. But those daggers of hers can probably make mincement of your webbing in short order.

Your strength returning with every second (add 2 Health points to your total), you bolt up the stairs.

Go to **209**.

You're gone. Deceased. Passed on. You **213** have shuffled off this mortal coil and joined the choir invisible. You are, in short, dead.

Might as well try the direct approach, **214** you decide. *The subtle approach never seems to work, anyway.* You go up to the door, check it over. There doesn't seem to be any sign of a booby trap—then again, you're just the booby to be trapped in this kind of instance.

But, nothing ventured, nothing gained. You kick open the door and spring in, looking for trouble. And find it.

Go to **236**.

"Blast and thunder," swears the silver- **215** haired woman. "He's gone—and I don't know where."

"A brilliant idea!" you say.

She turns to you hopefully. "What? What?"

"That's what we need, a brilliant idea."

She frowns. "You clearly do not appreciate the magnitude of the danger that's being faced. I'll have to find Stephen on my own, obviously—I don't need the aid of a jesting fool like you."

"Now wait just one min—"

She gestures and the air seems to swallow her up, leaving you standing there. You didn't exactly put your best foot forward with that one. Well, Silver seemed to know what she was doing, and you hope that she'll be able to pull this thing out of the fire. Chances are, she will. She's certainly better suited to this craziness than you are.

You hop up toward the skylight window in Doc's home, open it carefully and stand on the roof. The neighborhoods and streets of the city stretch out beyond.

This is your baliwick, this is where you're meant to be. The down and dirty reality of the city, not the interdimensional magics of Doc and company.

From somewhere in the distance, a woman shouts, "Stop, thief!"

"That's my cue," you say, and swing off into the night.

You leap forward, firing your webbing **216**
blindly, hoping that the quick move will somehow
catch Cloak (whom you presume is waiting for
you) off guard, and give you a brief advantage.

It's a nice idea, but it doesn't work, because before you know it, you're completely enveloped in
darkness.

Go to **237**.

You let out a long sigh. Add 3 Karma **217**
points to your total for accomplishing the deed
you set out to do.

Doc looks impatient, floating in front of you, but
for some reason something about him makes you
slightly short-tempered. "Cool your demons,
Doc," you say. "I just wanna make sure that everything is hunky-dorey."

From the inside of your elastic web cartridge belt
you withdraw the other two pieces of stone to
match with the third that you have in your hand.
They seem to grow more intense as you hold
them up, one toward the other, almost as if
they're striving to reach out and link with the others.

"What the heck," you say out loud and bring
them toward each other. There is a dazzling burst
of light and a feeling of incredible heat, and with a
yell, you drop the pieces to the ground.

They are individual pieces no longer. With a
loud "fwoosh," they have now linked together,
forming one solid piece—three-quarters of the
amulet that you've gone through so much to obtain.

It sits there smoldering in the dirt, the pieces
fused so completely that the seams are impossible

to spot. It's as if it were one solid piece that some-one had merely chipped a quarter out of, rather than three pieces rejoined.

You pick the amulet up slowly and look at Doc, who appears to be extremely perturbed with you. Then again, you suppose you can understand that. After all, you were just fooling around with a mystic thingamajig that could probably lay waste to the entire planet.

But then again, it's still incomplete. So it's kind of like fooling around with a hand grenade with-out pulling the pin.

"Okay, Doc," you say. "Take me home."

Go to **120**.

218   You manage to lift the Rhino over your head—and at that crucial moment, your strength gives way. You drop the Rhino—on top of yourself. He squishes you beyond repair.

You'll have plenty of time to pick up the pieces before you start the adventure over again.

219   Make an Agility FEAT roll. If the result is 12 or less, go to **165**. If the result is 13 or more, go to **190**.

220   Stepping back, you attach the amulet to a strand of webbing and then snap it forward like a yo-yo.

The amulet sails right into the middle of the barrier and there is a soundless explosion. You blink against the intensity of the light, and an un-earthly heat scorches your body.

And when the "dust" settles, the barrier is gone. You lunge forward, and see a doorway at the top of the stairs.

From behind you comes a voice, shouting, "Stay away from there! Mere mortals weren't meant to enter that room!"

Right, you think to yourself. *And while I'm at it I'll pay no attention to that man behind the curtain.*

Go to **38**.

The wind pushes against you now but, **221** putting your hand up in front of your face, you manage to block off some of its effects.

"Clea!" you call, stumbling forward. "Cle—" You practically stumble over her.

You crouch down next to her. Her chest is rising

175

and falling slowly—she's breathing. She's okay at the moment, but the two of you are going to have to get out of here soon or you could both die of frostbite or exposure.

The amulet is about the only thing you can think of that's going to be able to free Doc. You go over to the amulet and pick it up. Immediately, a warmth fills your body, a feeling of power unlike any you've ever felt. You don't feel the harshness of the wind anymore. You don't feel the fatigue you'd felt earlier. All in all, you feel like you could beat the world right now.

And you hear the voice in the back of your mind say, *Don't worry. Everything is going to be okay from now on.*

Go to **101**.

222 She stand there, waiting for you to make the first move, her arms frozen.

Make a Reason FEAT roll. If the result is 6 or less, go to **184**. If the result is 7 or more, go to **227**.

223 You've always been a direct kind of guy, and in this instance there's nothing better than the direct approach.

You launch yourself at the creature, making a Fighting FEAT roll. If the result is 9 or less, go to **171**. If it's 10 or more, go to **234**.

224 Make an Agility with Webbing FEAT roll. If the result is 18 or less, go to **69**. If the result is 19 or more, go to **39**.

You have now been completely stomped **225**
into little bits of nothing by the Rhino. You're not
in shape to as much as scratch your nose, much
less save the world. That's it for you.

It was a good theory, though.

You look up at Cloak, still perched on the **226**
top of the tower, and think, *Well—might as well
give the ground level a shot. He's sure going to
give me grief if I try going back up there.* Out loud,
you call, "Okay, Cloak! You win! I'm going home. I
mean, heck, the Mets are playing. Don't want to
miss that, right?" He doesn't reply.

You drop down to street level, landing easily
near the base of the tower.

Go to **214**.

227   *Hold it—I get it*, you say to yourself. *This whole defense mechanism in the spell—it doesn't do anything unless I make an attack move.*

But what if I don't make an attack move? The thing I've got on my side is that, if this is an accurate recreation of Dagger, I should be able to reason with her.

You sense Cloak seeping toward you, but you make no move against him either, staying frozen in place.

"Dagger," you say slowly, "you know me. Spider-Man. I know you're not a super-villain. You're a scared, mixed-up kid, a runaway. Both you and Cloak are. But there's no reason to fight me. I'm not one of the bad guys. I'm here to get a piece of something to avoid having the world reduced to a spinning ball of ashes."

She seems to be wavering slightly. "I'm not—the—enemy," you say carefully. "I'm on your side. Don't fight me—help me. Please. Like I helped you. Please."

Go to **21**.

228   You put everything you have into it, trying to push Seymour's head forward while maintaining the choke hold.

Seymour spins one way, then the other, furiously trying to shake you off. You try desperately to maintain your grasp but the creature is moving too quickly. It gets hard to concentrate—the world seems to spin about.

And then the creature manages to get a good grasp on your arm and locks onto it. He yanks and you howl, certain that the arm is about to be yanked out of its socket.

The creature pulls you off of itself and, with all its strength, slams you headfirst into the ground.

You go limp, consciousness escaping you.

Go to **112**.

Your aim is absolutely perfect as you **229** snag the quarter-amulet and yank it out of Mordo's grasp.

"Wait!" he shouts. "You don't know what you're doing!"

And as you pull the quarter toward you, reeling it in expertly, you say "Oh sure, that's what the bad guys always say right before I clobber 'em—"

As if it has eyes, the quarter-amulet sails across the room and lodges in the only open section left in the amulet. It fuses seamlessly.

You now hold the complete amulet.

"Okay, Mordo," you say. "You going to come quietly or do I hafta get rough—"

But you suddenly freeze in place, as if your entire body has been seized by rigor mortis. You can't speak, can't move—

Mordo is shouting something you can't quite hear and don't care about.

Go to **141**.

You leap to one side as bolts of eldritch **230** energy fill the room. You close your eyes, waiting to be turned into a frog, or some other ignominious fate.

Then you hear Doc swear, mentioning the names of some gods or creatures or something that you've never heard and somehow, with names like Dormammu and Satannish, you're

glad you've never met them.

You open your eyes and see that several bolts of mystic energy that appear to have your name on them fail to come in contact with you. You don't knock it, and immediately leap toward the only exit from the place—the stairway to the left.

Go to **38**.

231   Moving quickly, you try to bound out of the way of the light daggers, but they move just a hair too quickly. As if they have eyes, the daggers pass right through you and you go down.

"I'm sorry Spider-Man," says Dagger. The truly insane thing is that she sounds sincere. Subtract 5 Health points from your total.

Go to **212**.

The heck with it, you think. *He's just* **232** *one kid. I'm in the middle of something that has the whole world on the line. I just don't have time to spare for this.*

You swing off after Strange's floating image. The problem is that, even as you follow him, you feel a niggling disturbance in the back of your mind. Finally, you shout, "Doc! I can't stand it. I have to go back and stop that kid."

Doctor Strange's ectoplasmic form pauses in midair and starts to turn but you're already gone, swinging off in the direction that you saw the kid go.

Within moments, you've caught up, not with the kid, but with the woman he was running from. Her chest is heaving and she's sobbing to a police officer, "He got all my cash! My credit cards! Everything. I can't believe I didn't get traveler's checks—I never thought something like this would ever happen to me."

You grit your teeth, thinking that it wouldn't have happened if you'd used your head and gone after the kid when you had the opportunity. You swing around, checking out the area, but you can't find the kid anywhere.

Doc now floats in front of you, looking very impatient. You can't blame him. You can, however, blame yourself for shirking your responsibility. Deduct 1 Karma point from your total.

Go to **169**.

About sixty seconds later, there's rip- **233** pling in the air in front of you.

Doc Strange and Clea step through, and by the expressions on their faces and their tensed pos-

181

tures they are clearly ready for battle. You savor the shock that crosses their faces when they see you, sitting rather jovially on top of Mordo.

"Hi, kids," you say. "Sorry you got here so late. Boy," you note that their costumes are covered with rapidly melting snow, "where the heck were you guys?"

"The Himalayas," says Doc evenly.

"I, um, ran into some trouble," Clea puts in. "However it all disappeared—including the spell that was keeping Stephen a prisoner. Just vanished, about a minute ago."

"Ah yes," you say jovially. "That would be about the time I clobbered old Mordo here. Glad I could help out."

You toss Doctor Strange the final quarter of the amulet. He catches it and clearly takes care to

keep it separate from the rest of the talisman. "Keep this for your collection," you say.

"Thank you, Spider-Man," Doc says. "Thank you—for all your help."

You turn and look expectantly at Clea. She now looks extremely sheepish, but to her credit she pulls herself up and says, "Spider-Man . . . I thank you, too. It's clear that I misjudged you. Understand—when you come from a world of magic, you tend to feel rather pitying toward those who have no magical abilities."

"No magical abilities?" you retort. "I can stick to walls, and darned if I can figure out how I do it. If that's not magic, then I don't know what is."

Go to **242**.

The creature swings a huge, furry arm **234** that looks about the size of a truck. You duck under the clumsy lunge, however, and slam the creature in the pit of its stomach with the proportionate strength of a spider.

"What's the matter, Seymour?" you shout, not knowing or even caring if the thing understands what you're saying. "Can't stand the heat? Then get out of the freezer."

You hit Seymour again in the same place, and this time he doubles over. You continue with a double-fisted smash that catches him in the face. Seymour is knocked back, staggering, trying to clamber back to his feet. He's still got a lot of fight left in him, but in the meantime Clea might be freezing to death. You risk a quick glance at her and see that she is still not moving.

The creature lurches toward you, roaring. It's fetid breath alone could almost knock you over.

You have to end this quickly, you decide. Every passing moment, you feel yourself starting to slow down as the wind chills you more and more. Every second that passes tips the balance in Seymour's favor.

You clench your fist, summoning all your strength. Seymour approaches, and the snow and wind sap your power. Then you remember your webbing. You bring your hand up, and fire at Seymour's face, hoping to confuse him, blind him. But the wind blows the webbing away before it gets anywhere near him.

All right, then. So it'll have to be strength or nothing.

Make a Strength FEAT roll, adding Karma if you wish. If the result is 12 or less, go to **211**. If the result is 13 or more, go to **198**.

"I'm sorry, Spider-Man!" Dagger calls **235** out, as she unleashes her light weapons at you. They whiz through the air but you've already anticipating their course and you backflip over the barrage.

Seeing your chance, you bolt up the steps inside the tower, springing up with distance-consuming speed. Her footfalls are so light that you don't hear her, but you know Dagger is in hot pursuit.

Go to **209**.

Standing there is Dagger—and if Dagger **236** is there, Cloak can't be far behind.

But they're not bad guys, you think to yourself—except when you first met them, they were your opponents. Cloak and Dagger, two teen-aged runaways who became the victims of bizarre body- altering drugs.

Dagger is a stunningly beautiful young woman, clad in a white body-stocking. From her fingertips she is able to hurl light daggers. The most frequent targets of her assaults, drug users, find their bodies expunged of the horrors of drugs if they're hit by the daggers. For a fine, upstanding soul like yourself, though, they fill you with an almost paralytic numbness.

And she's about to hurl a few at you now!

No telling when her shadow-filled boyfriend is going to show up—you have to move quickly.

Make an Agility FEAT roll, adding Karma if you wish. If the result is 12 or less, go to **231**. If the result is 13 or more, go to **160**.

237   You've experienced this before, but that doesn't make it any easier. You realize immediately that you're trapped in the shadow realm of Cloak's darkness. You feel a chill cutting through you and you try to fight it off. You're disoriented, uncertain of where to go or what to do. A panic begins to fill you and you try to fight it off.

You shout at the top of your lungs but there's no sound.

Suddenly, from the darkness, hands reach out toward you, pulling at your body, tearing at your soul. You try to fight them off furiously, frantically.

"Get away!" you scream and at last you can hear yourself. You feel like your punching your way through jelly as you stagger farther into the blackness, not knowing where you're going, not caring. All that matters is getting away from where you are, to be somewhere else. Anywhere else.

At that moment, someone runs by you. You recognize the clothing almost immediately. It's the burglar. The burglar you let go those many years ago because you felt it wasn't your job to catch him. The burglar who repaid your non-interest by shooting down your beloved Uncle Ben in cold blood.

"Not this time!" you shout, trying to reach toward him. But you can't move. You're frozen as the blackness invades your innermost spirit and paralyzes you. The burglar vanishes into the darkness.

You wait for the inevitable and it comes— gunshots and a scream, the scream of your Aunt May as she witnesses her husband's death.

Go to **195**.

As the shadow rolls toward you, you **238**
leap in through the window, bracing yourself for
whatever you might find inside.

Facing you is Dagger. As always, you are momentarily stunned by her beauty. She's clad in a
white body stocking.

From her fingertips, she is able to hurl light daggers. The most frequent targets of her assaults,
drug users, find their bodies expunged of the horrors of drugs when they're hit by the light daggers. But for a fine, upstanding soul like yourself,
they fill you with an almost paralytic numbness.

And she's about to hurl a few at you now!

Go to **20**.

"Look, Silver," you tell her. "Before we **239**
go galavanting to who-knows-where looking for
Doc, maybe we should go back and check out his
house again."

Clea stares at you disbelievingly. "What? Why
would we want to do that? Mordo's gone. Stephen
is gone. And you want to waste valuable time
rooting around in an empty house when we have
the means at hand to track down Stephen?"

Make a Reason FEAT roll, adding Karma if you
wish. If the result is 9 or less, go to **186**. If the result is 10 or more, go to **240**.

"No," you say, now more assertive. "No, **240**
I want to go back to Doc's house, and I'll tell you
why—"

"He is not Doc," Clea says testily. "To you, he is
Doctor Strange and shall be addressed by his full

title, even when you're referring to him."

"Look, lady, this is New York, not the Dark Dimension. Maybe you're real hung up on titles out where you are, but we could care less about them around here."

"If you want to waste your time galavanting around an empty house when there's a man waiting to be rescued, you just go ahead and do that," Clea says. "Give me the amulet and I'll go my way and you go yours, and we won't have to worry about each other."

"Fine," you snap, tossing her the amulet. "Go ahead. Run off on a goose chase. See if I care."

"Your concern is extremely touching," she says haughtily. "Good day."

"Yeah, fine. Look, maybe you might still want to know that—" Clea, with a wave of her arms, vanishes into midair.

You slam your fist into your hand. "That's splendid," you say. "That's just beautiful. When am I going to learn to keep my big mouth shut and try to play well with the other kids?"

Go to **17**.

241   Doc is clearly waiting for a decision from you as to what you will do now. You stick the piece of amulet into your belt.

If you want to go to London, go to **111**.

If you want to go to Rome, go to **91**.

If all this is too weird for you, tell Doc you're packing it in, and go to **181**.

If you've gotten all three pieces of the amulet, then go to **217**.

"By the way, Doc," you say. "Shouldn't we try to find where Mordo has Wong stashed?"

Doc looks at you oddly. "Wong isn't here. He has personal matters to attend to."

"You mean Mordo actually told the truth about something?"

"Yes. It happens every so often."

You nod toward the amulet. "Whatcha gonna do with the magic thingy over there?"

"Ah, the amulet. I've given the matter some thought." He holds the amulet up. "It can't be destroyed by any physical or mystical means. The main thing is to make it inaccessible to anyone. However, there are means available to me that did not exist for my predecessors. I believe that I shall contact Reed Richards and ask him to rig a small, rocket-propelled device—he's quite clever at that

190

sort of thing. I'll place the amulet where it will eternally burn in the heart of a distant sun, inaccessible to all."

You sigh and lean against a wall. It's been an extremely draining experience—it's hard for you to believe that, in point of fact, all of this happened in a little less than a few hours. It's certainly been the most busy few hours that you can recall. If they had a frequent-flyer plan for people on mystical junkets, you'd have logged up enough miles for a free trip to Hawaii by now.

"You appear tired, my young friend," Doctor Strange observes.

You stare at him and, unable to resist, say, "Doctor, Mister M.D., can you tell me what's ailing me?"

And with an absolutely straight face, Doc finishes the lyric, "All you really need is true love."

You're aghast. "Doc! You made a funny."

"Did I?" he replies cooly. "I thought I was giving a prescription."

You think about it, then think about Mary Jane waiting for you, warm and loving, back at the apartment, and you say, "You know—I think maybe you're right at that."

You go to the front door, which opens by itself. You're not surprised. You step out, taking in a deep breath of air. Down the street, someone points and says, "Look! It's—what's his name!"

"That's me," you say agreeably. "The Amazing What's His Name."

Chuckling over the lack of fame you've accumulated, you fire a webline and swing off across the city toward Mary Jane and home.